DECORATE
A DOLL'S HOUSE

DECORATE
A DOLL'S HOUSE

AUTHENTIC PERIOD STYLES
FROM 1630 TO THE PRESENT DAY

MICHAL MORSE

The Lyons Press • New York

I should like to thank Faith Eaton for the
use of her extensive reference library, and
all the craftsmen whose work has
contributed to making this book as
authentic as possible.

First published in 2000 by
B T Batsford Ltd

A member of the Chrysalis Group plc

First Lyons Press edition, 2000

ISBN 1-55821-972-2

Designed by
Simon Rosenheim

Printed in Hong Kong

CONTENTS

INTRODUCTION

THE decoration of a doll's house is a very personal choice. It can be daunting to be faced with a bare wooden doll's house which needs painting and decorating throughout. There are so many decisions to be made. What period is the house? Is it to be inhabited in the present day, by people who collect antiques, or is it to be frozen in a time warp?

The easiest method is to collect furniture you like when you see it (you can never rely on finding the same piece months later) and date the house by the latest piece. A stone sink may be Victorian, or may still be used in the 1950s. Galvanized tin baths were still found in the 1950s in some cottages. A cast-iron bath with claw feet may be used in a Victorian doll's house, but full-size reproductions are on sale now. Once you have dated the furniture, you can dress the dolls to fit the period.

Alternatively you may plan the house around the family of dolls. If the house has less than six rooms you may have problems with the sleeping arrangements and plumbing. Conventional doll's houses are two or three storey and one room deep, with two rooms to each floor and a central hallway and staircase. The kitchen is usually on the bottom left. In reality the kitchen would not be near the front door of an elegant terraced house but 'below stairs' in the basement or at the back of the house insulated behind a

green baize door. I personally think no doll's house is complete without a kitchen and would never banish it behind an imaginary door.

This book will help you to recognize the characteristics of each period, and know the date of your own house or how you can adapt it. The same house can be completely transformed by the addition of bay windows or a porch, a brick finish, or roof detail.

A short history of housebuilding

The earliest houses were built of easily available local materials: upright posts interwoven with thinner branches and waterproofed with layers of mud. The simplest were circular and supported by a central post or even a tree, and thatched with straw, reeds, turves, or moss. Peasants in the twelfth and thirteenth centuries were still living in this type of flimsy 'wattle and daub' house. Easy to construct, they were also easily demolished as a punishment by the landowner for non-payment of dues or by a flitting tenant deciding to move house. In fact they

were so unstable they were liable to be blown over in a storm. Shepherds and their families built summer huts in this way, and charcoal burners were still building wattle and daub shelters up to the 1920s, using willow saplings from the clearings.

Some houses were built entirely of mud, known as cob, which was much more durable. I know of some old houses which were condemned as uninhabitable in the 1950s, but proved almost impossible to break down with pickaxes. In the days when roads were only dirt tracks (or thick mud in wet weather), people sometimes swept up and used road dust for housebuilding. Alternatively, local clay was mixed with chalk and a little straw to the consistency of a pudding mix, and this was piled on to a stone foundation and trodden down to form a

wall 2 ft wide and 3 ft high (60 x 90 cm). The wall was then left to dry for a week, with a layer of straw protecting the top. The next layer then soaked into the straw, which was trimmed flush when the wall was finished. Door frames and windows were fitted in as the work progressed, and the thatched roof was added once the walls were firm. The walls were protected by a band of tar along their base. Cob houses can still be seen in Devon and are easily recognized by their gently rounded corners, further softened by many layers of lime wash.

Traditional African round mud huts, or rendavels, are built in the same way, the thick walls providing better insulation from the hot sun than many modern materials. Sun-baked bricks are also used, made from a mixture of

Fig. 1 Simple circular stone house

clay and straw cast in wooden moulds.

Many of the most elegant buildings in Africa rely on a corrugated iron roof to keep out the heavy downpours of the rainy season.

Where stones were plentiful and wood scarce, simple domed dwellings were built with cantilevered stone roofs, or turf over woven branches (Fig 1). This stone igloo shape can still be seen in the Stone Age settlement of Scara Brae in the Scottish Orkneys. These compact houses have several rooms, with built-in cupboards and beds. The dry-stone walls were laid so that any rain would run off. Primitive stone huts were common in the west of Ireland, Wales and Scotland up to the fifteenth and sixteenth centuries, where the best way of clearing a field for cultivation was to use the stones for building a hut or for dry-stone walls.

With the development of tools in the Bronze Age (2,000 BC) larger timbers could be felled, and solid log hill forts and stockades like those of the Wild West were built. The remains of a tenth-century Royal Palace built for King Athelstan exist at

Cheddar in England. It is a very plain building with walls of upright tree trunks and a shallow pitched roof supported by gabled ends. The grand styles of the Roman occupation of Great Britain in AD 300-400, when stone was quarried for building construction, were long gone.

The use of solid timbers, known as blockwork, did not last in England as the forests were decimated, but log buildings can still be seen in Scandinavia and in central Europe in the coniferous forest belt (look at Black Forest huts and Swiss chalets). North American settlers also built log cabins as they cleared land. Wooden clapboard is still the most popular North American building material, but in England building with brick was encouraged by decree after the Great Fire of London in 1666, and it is still generally used, except in natural stone areas like the Cotswolds, Scotland and northern England.

Flimsy softwood houses did not

wide – enough to stable two pairs of oxen. Grain and hay were measured by the bay. A single bay cottage had two rooms: the main living room (with an open hearth) and a smaller room for sleeping. It could be extended by lean-to outhouses or by another bay.

town house. At first the upright posts, or studs, were spaced their own width apart, a practice known as 'post and pan', but as wood became harder to obtain they were spaced further apart.

Upright hazel wands were slotted between the horizontal beams and interwoven with split willow or sticks to form a strong hurdle infill which was then coated with a clay mix. This wattle and daub was protected with a layer of hair plaster (using horsehair or cows' tails), laid over thin slats nailed across the uprights. In England, many East Anglian houses had no exposed beams until recent 'restoration', as can be seen from nail holes left in the timbers. The plaster was often colour washed a strong ochre or Suffolk pink. The large expanses of wall were sometimes decorated with pargetting, a low relief decoration cast on the plaster.

survive, but stronger timbers used in their framework did and oak beams were often re-used in later houses. The first timber-framed cruck- or fork-buildings built in the fourteenth century were triangular in section, with a central beam, or ridge pole, supported on two pairs of timbers, each strengthened by a tie beam running across. The thatched roof curved almost to the ground, leaving a rather cramped living space. The next step was to extend the tie beams to support a shorter roof which rested on upright walls (Fig 2).

The upright or cruck beams were spaced in 'bays' about 16 ft (5 m)

The framework was jointed and pegged together on the ground before being hauled upright, and the base of the timbers were charred to prevent their rotting. The roofs were thatched with straw, reeds, rushes, or heather, or occasionally tiled with wooden shingles or burnt clay tiles. Wooden shingles are still popular in North America but have seldom been used in England since medieval times.

The walls were infilled with woven laths plastered with a mixture of clay, straw and cow-dung and the floors were beaten earth. A layer of lime wash every spring disinfected the house.

With the growing independence of tenants and yeoman farmers from the mid-sixteenth to the mid-seventeenth century, sturdy two-storey houses were built, their wooden frames resting on low foundations of brick or stone. Sometimes the top floor was jettied to project over the ground floor, which gave more space - particularly for a

Fig. 2 Cruck House

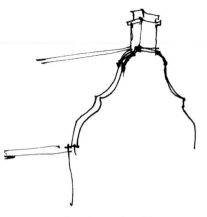

Fig. 3 Dutch gable

Sometimes the plaster was finished flush with the beams, leaving the timber exposed. The timber was then left to weather to a silvery grey or sometimes whitewashed with the walls. As oak took years to season, it was used green and where it warped the walls had to be filled - today there remain some extraordinarily crooked houses. The so-called ships' timbers used in many of these old houses were usually curved naturally.

Stone cottages and houses continued to be built where stone was available. Simple single storey dwellings developed into substantial two and three storey houses. In limestone areas stones were split to form roof tiles.

Most roofs were tiled; thatch was forbidden in large towns after the thirteenth century because of the fire risk. The tiles were fired locally, and bricks, previously imported but seldom used in the Middle Ages, were made for chimney stacks. Some small manor houses were built entirely of brick. Much larger still, Hampton Court Palace was built by Cardinal Wolsey between 1515 and 1525. It is a grandiose building with terracotta

decorations and soaring chimneys. When Wolsey was disgraced, Henry VIII promptly commandeered the palace that had threatened his authority.

After the Great Fire of London houses were rebuilt in brick and stone, though Christopher Wren's grand designs for rebuilding the City of London were never completed. There had been other fires which spread quickly through the overhanging wooden houses, but this was the worst.

New designs began to appear. Classical designs came over from Italy, influenced by Palladio, with solid Doric columns, fluted Ionic, and delicate Corinthian with acanthus leaf capitals. Longleat, the Marquess of Bath's Wiltshire mansion, was built between 1546-80 in the classical style.

Inigo Jones was an important architect in the early seventeenth century. He designed the Piazza and the Church of St Paul's in Covent Garden, London, the latter with a triangular pediment supported by four pillars. Unfortunately he forgot that all churches face east, and the impressive door is blocked inside by the altar. The entrance is through a quiet courtyard on the west side!

As Dutch Protestants fled the Continent in the seventeenth century, they influenced the architectural

styles. Red brick houses with curved Dutch gables can still be seen in East Anglia (Fig 3). Queen Anne (1702-1714) houses, also red brick, tend to have large hipped roofs (with no side gables but triangular roof panels sloping back to the ridge) with deep overhanging eaves (Fig 4).

In the eighteenth century, the Georgian period was known for the classical symmetry of its elegant buildings, built of stone, stone and brick, and later of stone simulated by a cement finish. Then came the Victorians with their varied styles, from the mock-baronial halls built by opulent businessmen to the

Fig. 4 Queen Anne house with hipped roof

vernacular (local style) country cottages designed by Lutyens at the end of the nineteenth century.

The love of mock-Tudor continued into the 1930s, and even now there are some remarkable estates springing up with a variety of nostalgic features – Tudor beams, tile hanging, and Georgian doors all make frequent appearances. There seems to be no recognizable contemporary style. The geometric patterns of the 1930s influenced the building of flat-roofed houses, really more suitable for drier climates. Doll's houses of the period copy these styles, either mock-Tudor or flat-roofed with pebbledash walls.

Until recently, doll's houses were built in contemporary styles, maybe ten years behind the times. They reflected the date of the owner's real house when first married which was then copied for the children. Now it is hard to find modern doll's houses or furniture; there is a nostalgia for the past, extending even to the 1930s. The examples that follow are planned as an introduction to the typical styles of architecture, decoration, furniture, and costume of the Stuart, Georgian, Victorian, Edwardian and 1930s periods. The doll's houses are all built to the scale of 1/12th (1 in: 1 ft), the scale used for serious collectors of all ages. The ideas can be easily adapted to suit your own doll's house.

CHAPTER ONE

Tudor house furnished in Stuart style, 1630s

A side panel opens to show the parlour and kitchen of a timber-framed Tudor house, showing life in the 1630s. The steeply sloping roof may have originally been thatched.

The front panel opens to show the bedroom and living room. The exterior woodwork has weathered to a greyish colour.

THIS sturdy timber-framed house could have been built in the sixteenth or seventeenth centuries, although the style is generally referred to as Tudor. By Victorian times these houses had often deteriorated into damp hovels, and those that survived have been lovingly restored in the twentieth century.

The earliest windows were not glazed – they were merely openings, or wind-outs, to release smoke from the central fire before the use of chimneys. They were usually near the ceiling and were not used for seeing out. Sliding shutters covered the windows. Some exterior shutters hinged down, and were used by shopkeepers to display their wares.

Oiled linen, parchment and horn were used to cover small windows, the horn being boiled to soften it so it could be flattened. Blown glass had been made since Roman times, but it was not generally used for windows until the early seventeenth century. The panels were no more than 25 x 15 in (63 x 38 cm), being cut from a cylinder that was split then flattened.

Doors were simple, made of upright planks joined by two horizontals across the back, or even planked right across the back (Fig 5). Important doors often had decorative iron studs and were set in a doorway with a double radius arch (Fig 6). The strap hinges were on the inside of the door. If seen on the outside the door must open outwards, which is unusual.

The framework of the house was built of timbers at least 1 ft (30 cm) square, and 6 in (15 cm) posts or uprights. The wattle and daub infill was covered with plaster and whitewashed or colour washed. This

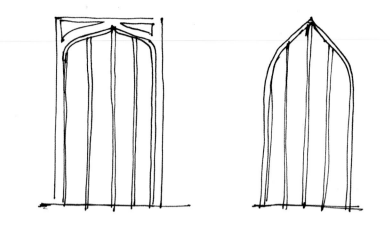

Fig. 6 Double radius arch

Fig. 5 Planked doors

houses of yeoman farmers and the gentry had close studding.

Square framing was used for poorer houses and sheds. A natural curve in the wood might be used decoratively, the two halves used on opposite corners as arch-bracing to support a cross beam, or as truss-bracing joining an upright and its base support.

The first floor is supported on joists which can run across the room, supported by a girding beam in the wall, or run the length of the house between the bays. Extra bridging beams can be used if the rooms are too wide. The floorboards are laid across the joists. Originally left open so the heat from the fire could warm the bedroom, the ceilings were later plastered between the joists or up to the bridging beams.

Fires were originally lit on stone slabs in the centre of the house and smoke escaped through the roof, which, being unlined, had plenty of ventilation. Louvres were sometimes fitted. Later the fire was moved to one end of the hall and a timber-framed smoke hood tapered to a hole or a chimney in the roof. Although lined with plaster this was rather inflammable, so brick was often painted right across the timbers. In East Anglia the houses were usually plastered all over to protect the woodwork, and decorative patterns of curves or flowers were combed or stamped in the plaster. In richer households the infill was brick, either laid flat or laid in a herringbone pattern. Further protection was given by tile hanging on the top floor and weatherboard (or clapboard), overlapping planks of wood about 6 in (15 cm) wide.

The more important, expensive

Fig. 7 Tudor thatch with decorative ridge

Living room, with pewter displayed on the oak buffet and a table-carpet covering the dining table

chimneys were introduced, supported on brick piers and a cross beam. Hearths were laid with brick.

In the time of the hall house, master and servants ate in one room at the same table, the master at the head of the table, the rest in decreasing order of importance. A large, decorative salt cellar indicated the division between servants and family or guests (hence the expression 'below the salt'). By the sixteenth and seventeenth centuries the master ate separately from his staff.

The house on page 13 has a soft colour wash and greyish timbers. The circular framework and stone-flagged floor would be seen in the Midlands. The leaded windows in the gable project, and the walls are close studded (post and pan). Both are signs of a prosperous owner. The roof ridge has sunk slightly, showing that the house is no longer new, it could be Elizabethan. It could have been thatched (Fig 7), in which case the reeds or straw would have weathered to a dark brown. (Use coconut fibre if you'd like to try this and colour it with paint or wood stain.)

Living room

This house has a large inglenook fireplace in the main room. A cast-iron fireback protects the brick wall and a log fire is supported on a pair of firedogs. The uprights stop the logs rolling forward. As fires were difficult to light (matches were not made until Victorian times, so a light had to be struck by a tinder striking iron with the spark igniting a wick), they were usually kept burning all winter. Some were even kept alight for a hundred years! At night they were covered with an

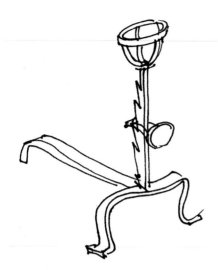

*Fig. 8 Firedog with ratchet
for spit and cup holder*

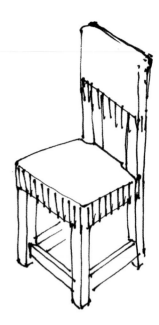

Fig. 9 Upholstered chair

iron hood called a curfew to keep a low fire burning and stop any sparks causing damage.

A joint of meat is roasting on a spit on its own set of firedogs. Some dogs have a ratchet that will support a spit on varying levels (Fig 8) or a round cup holder for warming drinks. A smoke jack in the chimney turns the spit. These were previously turned by hand or by a dog in a small wheel on the wall. The logs are piled up on a heap of ash, which retains the heat. (This can be made from real ash or coloured polyfilla mixed with wood glue, with a scattering of chopped red sequins which will gleam like embers.)

A pewter chandelier hangs over the table and another in the parlour. Similar wall brackets may be used throughout the house, plain wood or iron in the kitchen. Floor-standing candlesticks can be moved around. A lantern clock hangs by the fire and an hour-glass is used for time-keeping in the parlour.

An oriental carpet covers the table. These were far too valuable to lay on the floor, which may have been covered with rush matting similar to that still imported today and always useful on damp stone floors. A white cloth was laid over the carpet at mealtimes.

Most people carried their own knife, for cutting meat, and a spoon for eating small pieces, 'spoon meat' and soups, which could also be drunk out of small posset cups (two-handled bowls). Anything else was eaten with the fingers, and the diners washed their hands when a servant brought round a ewer and basin.

Early plates were made from flat wooden boards called trenchers, or sometimes from a hard baked bread. Drinking vessels were made of horn and leather, and earthenware pottery, which was also used for bowls and serving dishes, and sometimes decorated with a line of white clay slip. Once pewter was available, wood and pottery were banished to the kitchen. The pewter, or solid silver in grand houses, was displayed on a cup-board, a stepped structure covered with a cloth which later became simply a storage space with doors. The buffet is used here to display dishes and plates, goblets, jugs and tankards. Beer and ale (made from barley and oats without hops) were brewed at home and were a safe drink for the whole family at a time when water was likely to be contaminated. A bellamine jug on the table would hold beer for the master.

He sits in a heavy oak armchair. The rest of the family might sit on benches or stools, or early chairs known as 'back-stools'. Those with flat wooden seats had fat tapestry cushions. Other chairs were covered in leather or velvet (Fig 9), but

upholstery was seldom padded before the 1670s.

Food was either boiled or roasted over an open fire, or sometimes baked in a covered pan or in an earthenware pot set on a low fire or in the ashes. A bread oven was sometimes built outside on to the back of the chimney, and separate outhouses were used for the dairy and the wash house.

The washing might be done out of doors, with a fire lit under a free-standing tank of water, or in a nearby stream, and there was much beating of clothes to extract the dirt. Soap (lye) was a mixture of ash and fat. In the country, sheets and linen were laid over bushes (preferably lavender) to bleach in the sun.

Kitchen

The food preparation and wet work or washing were always kept separate from the cooking. In this house, the right-hand room can be

In the solar, or parlour, the mistress of the house can entertain her friends on the mandolin, work on a tapestry, spin her own wool. She also works hard in the kitchen with her maid, making butter and cheeses, brewing ale, kneading bread to be baked in an outdoor oven.

The bedroom has a carved oak four-poster bed with 'crewel' work curtains and an embroidered coverlet

used for the dairy and bread preparation. Bowls of milk and cream would be laid out on stone slabs, and the bread dough kneaded in a wooden trough and left to rise under muslin covers. Cheeses are stored on shelves, and all food is kept in wooden tubs or hung out of reach of rats among bunches of herbs drying on the beams.

Slices of toast or fried bread were served with soups and stews. Potatoes were sometimes used in stews, but not as separate vegetables. A wide variety of home-grown fruit and vegetables were available, including melons and tomatoes ('love apples'). Sugar and oranges were imported.

Parlour

The mistress of the house has her parlour, or solar, on the floor above where she can sew and spin and entertain friends. She might play a lute or mandolin. There is a tapestry on the wall, and the little girl stands by an embroidery frame. The locked spice cabinet contains drawers of valuable herbs and spices, many imported from the East Indies. A carved court cupboard is used for storage, and a food hutch with ventilation holes in its doors stands near the window. The toddler is supported in a baby walker.

Bedroom

The master bedroom is luxurious in having a fireplace, but thick hangings on the four-poster bed keep out the draughts. A single window curtain, pulled to one side, would be used to keep out the sunlight. The four-poster bed would probably have a straw mattress covered by one of felt and then a feather bed, which was one loose bag of feathers without stitching. The bed could be aired with hot embers in a solid brass warming pan. The linen sheets would be spun from locally grown flax or hemp and woven by the mistress. A coarser fabric was sometimes made from nettles, hence the fairy story of the swan princes whose spell was broken by garments of nettles. There is an embroidered coverlet, and the hangings might be crewel work (embroidered wool on linen). These hangings are made from a floral brocade.

A chest of drawers with raised panels and a chest are used for clothes. A flint box and candlestick might be kept on a joint stool by the bed. The painting hangs out from the wall at an angle. The mirror's frame would be carved and gilded wood. Silver gilt was also used later in the century. There is a hooded cradle and a solid wooden rocking horse. The children might sleep on a truckle bed pulled out from beneath the bed.

Costume

The family are dressed in Stuart style, about 1630-40, with lace collars instead of ruffs, and the gentlemen still wear stockings and baggy trousers. This date allows for a variety of furniture; Elizabethan furniture would be limited to a bed, a chest, a table and some benches. In the time of the Commonwealth, from 1649-1660, Puritan dress was simple. The women wore sober colours, with a flat white collar and cuffs, and a plain cap covering their hair. The men wore black clothes and tall hats and were known as Roundheads because of their cropped hair. Royalists, both men and women, wore their hair in ringlets and dressed in velvet with lace at the neck and cuffs.

CHAPTER TWO

Stone cottage, nineteenth-century furnishing

Interior of a stone cottage built in the 1600s, the rustic furniture unchanged through the 18th to the 19th century

SOME of the earliest houses were built of stone using local materials - either uncut rocks picked up from the ground or rocks quarried without being trimmed square. A cottage's dry-stone walls were sealed inside with mud to stop the draughts. The roof was thatched with turf, heather, reeds or straw laid over inter-woven rods.

In Spain and the west of Ireland the roofs are often inset between the side walls. Spanish roofs have curved pantiles, set in cement (Fig 10). In Ireland the thatch is weighted down with rocks and ropes to withstand the Atlantic gales. Originally the only light came in through the doorway, which was covered with a cloth or skins when the weather was cold. The floors were hard beaten earth, sometimes sealed with chalk or bullocks' blood.

In Britain the limestone belt running from Lincolnshire to Dorset has produced elegant Georgian houses in Bath, built of ashlar (square cut) blocks, and mellow Cotswold villages, where houses are built of random stone or ashlar with stone-tiled roofs. Further north the red sandstone of Cheshire is used for important villas, corporation buildings, and high garden walls. The grey granite of Northumberland and Scotland is used for plain farmhouses, and

Fig. 10 Spanish house with pantiles

Fig. 11 Stone mullions with drip mould

Fig. 12 Planked door with diagonals

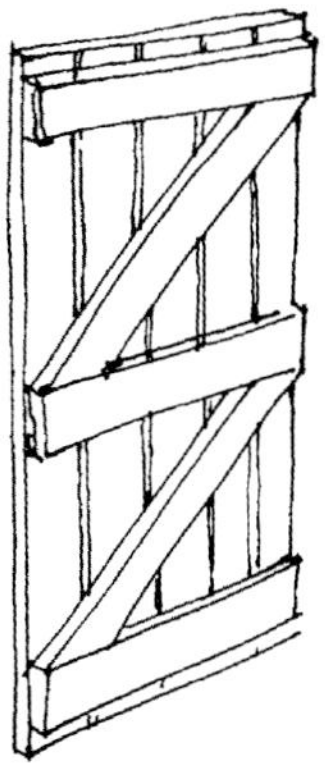

Fig. 13 Gothic pediment over two radius arch

solid tenement buildings for low-cost housing.

The house pictured is based on a seventeenth-century Cotswold cottage, built of random stone and laid in rough layers in a soft lime mortar (a mixture of lime, sand and very little cement). The walls are 2 ft (60 cm) thick, and the door and window openings are supported by sturdy timber lintels. The stone window sills project slightly. The sides of the openings and the corners of the building are lined with alternate ashlar blocks, like quoins, but flush. More important houses would have a shaped 'eyebrow' above the top of the window as a drip moulding, and chamfered stone mullions (uprights) (Fig 11).

Early front doors were planked, with upright planks outside and horizontal planks inside. Lighter

internal doors were held together by three cross-pieces and two diagonals, with the top of the diagonal away from the hinge to give strength to the door (Fig 12). Split doors or stable doors were more often used for the back door; open the top to let the light in, close the bottom to keep the children in, and the chickens and draught out.

The stone door surround sometimes had a gently curved arch (a two radius arch), with the two corners having a tighter arc than the gentle curve of the top. An important doorway could have a Gothic pediment (Fig 13).

A wide variety of windows can be used – choose mullion, casement, side sash (Figs 14–16), many paned Georgian sash or plain Victorian.

The low roof of this house comes down to the ground floor ceiling, so

the dormer window could be a later addition. A window could be cut in the gable without a chimney, but this will not light the whole attic. Some stone roofs are set within the gable walls, but most finish almost flush with the outside wall, set in a waterproof bed of cement with a small overhang at the eaves. Before the addition of guttering, the rain dripped evenly over the edge – which may be better than having a faulty gutter that pours the water down one section.

Stone roof tiles are made by splitting stone to about $^1/_4$ – $^1/_2$ in (6–13 mm) thick, and they are graded in size from about 24 in (60 cm) high at the bottom to 6 in (15 cm) at the top - roofers have a special measuring stick marked in graded sizes. Slats are nailed horizontally across the rafters, and

Fig. 14 Wooden mullions

Fig. 15 Casement window

Fig. 16 Side sash window

Living room with simple furniture, and stone seats built into the inglenook fireplace, with hams hanging from the ceiling.

the slates drilled and pegged. Metal pegs are used now – they were originally wood, or sheep's bones.

Before the use of tarred felt the roofs were insulated by setting the tiles in a bed of clay (when my own roof was rehung, clouds of dust covered the neighbours for months). This kept them firm and filled the gaps. When sometimes the whole roof is set in cement, the tiles can never be re-used, and it is difficult to repair. The shaped ridge tiles are cemented, and most angled joints – the gullies and the join of a dormer – are still set traditionally in cement (Figs 17 and 18). A skilled tiler can interleave two slopes, hiding a fillet of lead.

Chimneys are built either of rubble with ashlar corners, or completely of ashlar. Various additions were made to stop the smoke being blown back down the chimney. There may be a flat slab across the top supported on a couple of 4 in (10 cm) blocks or three or four slates set vertically across the hole as a windbreak. (I have an antique doll's house of a stone town house with that detail.)

The smoke from a 6 ft (2 m) wide inglenook fireplace cannot be constricted with chimney pots without considerable blow-back. As long as there are plenty of draughts, and the room is not hermetically sealed as so often the case nowadays, the fire should draw without smoking as long as it is kept well back from the hearth. Sometimes a 12 in (30 cm) pelmet filled the top of the opening to restrict the smoke.

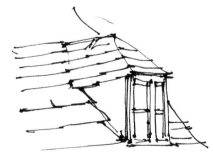

Fig. 17 Hipped dormer

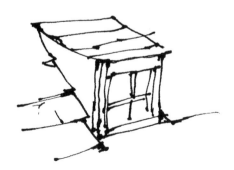

Fig. 18 Pent roofed dormer

Living room

This cottage has two downstairs rooms. One has to be the living room or the 'houseplace', with its fire. The other could be the sleeping quarters, the parlour, or for food preparation and storage. The walls are plastered and lime-washed, the floor stone-flagged.

The inglenook fireplace is built into the thickness of the end wall (if it were a later addition it would have been built on to the outside wall). Stone quoins support the lintel. A door to the side of the fire opens into a spiral stone staircase. You will find the same design, in wood, in a timber-framed cottage.

The walls would be 2 ft (60 cm) thick, the window openings angled to let more light into the room. Sometimes the recess continues to the floor, allowing space for a cupboard, or forms a window seat or a very deep window sill set into the plastered walls (Fig 19). This doll's house, however, has been kept simple, and $^3/_8$ in (10 mm) walls used throughout.

The living room is simply furnished, with an oak dresser, a solid wooden armchair, a table and some stools. A high-backed chair can be moved nearer the fire. A settle could be used to keep out the draught. The cooking is done over the open fire; a cauldron for stew or hot water can be suspended by

chains at the back of the fire or hung on a crane at the side. Smaller pans stand on trivets or on their own feet in the embers. A spit rack above the fire can hold the spits not in use and a shotgun or old blunderbuss (which was loaded with anything that could be crammed down its barrel).

I have cooked like this in a Dordogne farmhouse, boiling a kettle over brushwood in twenty minutes. It is all right for a holiday, but flicking an electric switch is much easier!

A bread oven is built into the far side of the fire, its cast-iron door set across the corner. It is heated by burning faggots, and when it is hot enough the ashes are swept out and the bread dough pushed in on a wooden peel – a paddle-shaped bat. As the oven cools down other food such as pies can be put in. Hams are hung at the back of the fire to smoke and are blackened with soot. Others

hang from beams in the ceiling.

This setting could be unchanged for about two hundred years. I have seen a photograph of a turf fire in the 1930s that had been burning for a hundred years! Cottage folk did not go in for upholstered furniture; with their muddy clothes and ever-present livestock it would have been difficult to keep clean. However, the shaped wooden seats and angled chair backs were well designed for comfort, and the stone-flagged floor can be covered in home-made rugs.

Parlour

When there was a parlour it was used for special occasions – on Sundays, or for laying out a coffin (hence the later name of coffin stools for joint stools). In Victorian times the room would be crammed with ornaments under glass domes,

Attic store room used for preserving apples, onions, herbs, with crocks of salted vegetables and jars of home brewed ale and wine

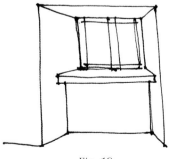

Fig. 19
Angled window set in deep wall

The bedroom has chests for storing clothes and a three-legged 'cricket' table, designed to stand level on an uneven floor. The double bed has a straw mattress, and would have been assembled in the attic.

The copper in the corner of the kitchen has a huge cast iron bowl set in bricks over a fire, and is used for washing clothes, which are stirred with the wooden washing dolly.

treasured heirlooms, pictures, photographs and trousseau lace; sometimes relics of a grander past from a woman who had married beneath her, or gifts from rich employers to those in service. Births, deaths and marriages would be recorded in the front of the family Bible.

Kitchen

You could furnish the right-hand room as a parlour, and imagine or build 'outshuts' for storage and washing. In this doll's house the room is a kitchen, with a copper and a sink, and some washing is strung across the ceiling to dry. In good weather it would hang outdoors. A basket of eggs and vegetables from the garden are ready for market. Pottery crocks and wooden tubs are used for storage and a jar of cider sits on a side table.

Bedroom

The attic bedroom is cramped; a little more headroom is given by the dormer. The second room, now the children have left, is used for storage. It was quite usual for a cottager to rear ten children in a house of this size.

The bedroom will be warmed by the heat from the chimney, and by some heat rising through the floor. The plain double bed has a straw mattress, and a coarse blanket under a knitted patchwork cover. On a cold night a brick heated in the fire would be wrapped in a cloth as a foot warmer. A chest at the end of the bed holds the clothes. A curtain would cover the opening to the end room, where barrels of apples, strings of onions, jars of preserved salted vegetables and home-brewed wines and dried herbs are stored away from the damp of the kitchen.

The old couple are dressed in simple Victorian style. The man could be a farm labourer or a smallholder. He has some chickens, sheep, and a goat. His wife will take produce to the local market once a week: cheese, butter, vegetables and eggs.

Exterior

Any four-room house can be painted to resemble stone. A more formal one would have square cut stones (ashlar) instead of random rubble. Use two tones of paint to indicate stonework. Cut stone roof tiles from thin card, ply or cork sheet.

MAKING AND DECORATING THE HOUSE

If you want to make this cottage rather than decorating a ready-made one, the following directions are adapted from my book Build a Doll's House. The cottage shown was cut down from a kit. Built of $^3/_8$ in (10 mm) plywood or MDF, the finished house is 26 in wide × 12 in deep × 20 in high (166 × 30 × 50 cm). If you prefer to make thicker walls you can build up hollow walls of $^1/_8$ in (3 mm) ply on a $^3/_4$ in (19 mm) frame. Batten the windows top and bottom, cutting the battens to an angle to the side panels to make a larger opening inside (Fig 20). If the recess continues to the floor the bottom battens fit on either side of the opening.

You will need:

- 8 × 4 ft (2.44 × 1.22 m) sheet of $^3/_8$ in (10 mm) MDF or plywood (most wood merchants will cut panels to size), or Basic House kit
- 1 × 2 in (25 × 51 mm) balsa, or strip wood (for stairs and inglenook seats)
- 1 × 4 × 12 in (2.5 × 10 × 30 cm) balsa (for chimney)
- card, thin ply or cork sheet (for stone tiles) and card (for inglenook)
- moulded flagstones (optional)
- $^1/_2$ in (13 mm) square strip wood (for beams)
- $^1/_4$ in (6mm) ply for dormer
- planked doors and hinges
- medium brown woodstain
- charcoal
- emulsion paint sample pots: drab, bone, mahogany, off-black, olive, old white (Farrow & Ball)
- wood glue
- $^3/_4$ in (19 mm) or 1 in (25 mm) panel pins
- mini drill or awl
- masking tape
- jig or hand saw
- drill
- small tenon saw
- hinge or hooks (for front)
- hammer and pin punch

Fig. 20 Battens for thick wall

CONSTRUCTION

Adapt the kit, or build the cottage following the instructions below.

1 Cut panels of $^3/_8$ in (10 mm) ply or MDF to the sizes given:
   - Back and front panels: 10 x 26 in (25.4 x 66.6 cm)
   - Two side panels: 16 $^3/_8$ in high x 12 in (41.6 x 30.5 cm). Cut the roof angles from the centre top to within 10 $^3/_8$ in (36.4 cm) of the bottom.
   - Cut approx 2 in (5 cm) off the top of the left wall.
   - Floor: 12 x 25 $^1/_4$ in (30.5 x 64 cm). Base: 12 $^3/_8$ x 26 in (31.4 x 66.6 cm)
   - Roof panels: 10 $^3/_4$ x 26 $^1/_2$ in (27.3 x 67.3 cm)(front) & 10 $^3/_8$ x 26 $^1/_2$ in (26.4 x 67.3 cm)(back)
   - Two internal walls: 8 $^5/_8$ x 12 in (21.9 x 30.5 cm)
   - Attic wall: 9 $^1/_2$ x 8 $^5/_8$ in (24 x 21.9 cm) cut to fit back slope and part of front
   - Front base: 2 $^1/_2$ x 26 in (6.4 x 66 cm)
   - Chimney: cut later approx 5 x 3 in (12.7 x 7.6 cm) to fit balsa

2 Check for fit, then tape back, sides and base with masking tape. Support the floor on two walls.

3 Tape front and roof, not forgetting the base underneath the front (Fig 21).

Cutting the openings

1 Take the panels apart and cut a hole 2 $^3/_4$ x 5 in (7 x 12.7 cm) in the ceiling for the stairs.

2 Cut the doorway and window openings, cutting internal doorways $^3/_8$ in (10 mm) from the front edge. You can add another window and a back door, but they will cut down on the space left for furniture. The planked doors are 6 $^1/_2$ x 2 $^1/_2$ in (16.5 x 6.4 cm) and will fit the staircase.

3 Cut the inglenook in one internal wall, cutting a hole 4 x 4 in (10 x 10 cm) which is slightly curved at the top, 2 $^1/_2$ in (6.4 cm) from the back edge.

4 The dormer will be cut out of the roof later.

Painting the panels

1 Paint the panels before assembly. The inside walls and ceiling are a dirty white emulsion, or can be colour washed with a pale mixture of yellow ochre and white. Add sooty streaks above the fire, on the ceiling and in the corners. Black mixed with white will go blue-grey, so rub or stipple dry colours. Real soot, charcoal or pastel rubbed on with

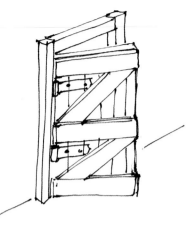

Fig. 22 Set door back

your finger is ideal. The final effect can be added when assembled.

2 The attic floor is of pale, scrubbed boards. Draw lines at least $^3/_4$ in (19 mm) apart with a soft pencil and brown felt-tip pen.

3 Flagstones can be painted on the floor now, or a precast sheet added later. Draw uneven slabs about 1$^1/_2$ x 2 in (38 x 50 mm) and paint in several tones of mixed black, white and ochre, or an almost even cream colour for a well-scrubbed floor. Then paint the lines between the flags. Remember that part of the floor will be covered by the inglenook.

4 The exterior stonework can be either darker or lighter than the mortar. You can paint a cream base and paint in darker stones (sometimes quite green with moss), or paint darker mortar and slightly varied stones. Although the stones are uneven, they are laid in rows. Thicker paint mixed up with polyfilla and glue can be palette-knifed on to the walls after the house has been assembled.

5 Paint the lintels to resemble grey weathered wood, or cut uneven strips of veneer.

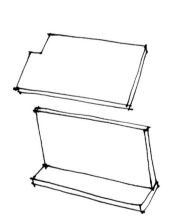
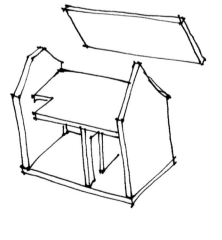

Fig. 21 Construction of stone cottage

6 Fit the window frames. They can be painted a stone colour to look like weathered paintwork.

7 Add shallow window sills, painted to match the stonework.

8 Hang the front door. It can be set back and hung on uprights behind the opening (Fig 22). Use strap hinges, if possible, painted black.

Stairs

1 Cut steps from solid wood, or more easily from balsa, or build up treads and risers cut from thin ply or sheet (Fig 23). Work out how many steps you need to reach the next floor.

Inglenook with cooking crane

This height of 9 in (23 cm) took 11 steps – the top one only $^3/_8$ in (10 mm) plus the floor. These were cut from 1 in (25 mm) balsa and carved to resemble worn stone steps. Build the two flights separately, 2 $^3/_4$ in (7 cm) wide for the bottom, 2 $^1/_2$ in (6.4 cm) wide for the top by 2 $^3/_4$ in (7 cm) deep and carve away the back of the top flight to make room for the inglenook seat.

2 Glue the stairs together, and try against the inglenook wall.

Inglenook

1 Make the curved recesses, and two seats 1 in (2.5 cm) high. You can use

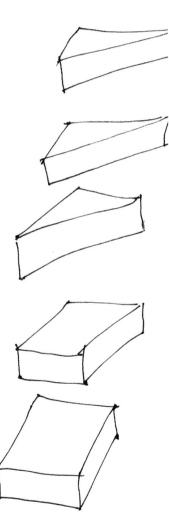

Fig. 23 Circular stone staircase

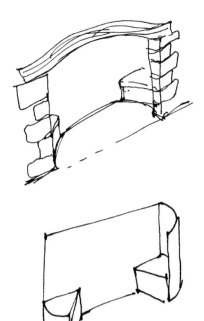

Fig. 24 Inglenook seats

the inside of a toilet roll (also useful for making tub chairs). The seats are canted into the fireplace, the backs are curved and they butt up to the back wall of the fireplace (Fig 24).

2 Cut the left-hand seat to fit under the stairs. Join both seats to a rigid back of $^1/_8$ in (3 mm) ply or sheet. Glue stairs and seats to the inglenook wall and check against the opening in the ceiling.

House assembly

1 Pin and glue the base to the back. Drill small pilot holes in the base from the side to be joined and pin with $^3/_4$ in (19 mm) or 1 in (25 mm) panel pins. (You could also use $^3/_4$ in (19 mm) no.4 countersunk screws if you pre-drill into both panels to avoid splitting.)

2 Pin and glue a $^1/_2$ in (13 mm) square beam, stained and chamfered, to the right-hand wall to support the ceiling.

3 Fix the sides, keeping square with

the ceiling and internal wall (Fig 25).

4 Pin and glue the internal wall to
   the back and floor, after fixing the
   door in place if necessary.

5 Fix the fireplace wall.

6 Fix the ceiling in place, resting on
   the beam and pinned to the
   internal wall and the fireplace. If
   not already drawn lay attic
   floorboards about $^3/_4$ – 1 in (19-25
   mm) wide. They are pale, well
   scrubbed and sanded.

Front

Join the front to the front base. This
can be cut to an irregular shape, paved
or grassed. Hinge, or add hooks to
both sides.

Chimney

1 Cut a block of 1 x 3 in (2.5 x 7.6 cm)
   timber or balsa 12 in (30.5 cm)
   high. Position, with a $^3/_8$ in (10
   mm) chimney panel fitting the
   outside wall (Fig 26). Try both roofs
   against it, mark them and cut to fit.

2 Pin and glue the back slope. Fit the
   front roof, taping if necessary.

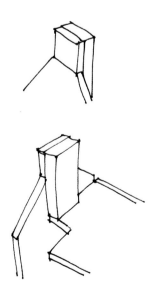

Fig. 26 Chimney

Fig. 25 Assemble house

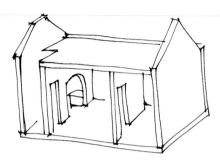

Dormer

1 Cut a triangle of $^1/_4$ in (6 mm) ply or
   MDF for the dormer; a 9 in (30 cm)
   base by 8 in (20 cm) high was used.
   It should be a similar angle to the
   gable. Mark where it will fit on the
   eaves. Take a straight line back to
   the roof from the apex, then draw
   the angle to the eaves (Fig 27).

2 Cut two right-angled triangles from
   card to fit the measurements of the
   slope of the dormer front, the
   distance from the apex to the roof
   and the slope down. Tape the
   dormer together and draw its
   position on the roof before cutting
   away $^1/_4$ in (6 mm) inside the line, to
   allow for joining. Cut two roof panels
   from $^1/_4$ in (6 mm) ply or MDF using
   the card as a pattern.

3 Fit a window into the triangle after
   painting it to match the wall.

4 Paint the front edges and overhang
   of the roofs before assembling.

5 Glue the roofs on the triangle and at
   the ridge, using $^1/_4$ in (6 mm) strip to
   strengthen the inside of the ridge,
   and keep firm with masking tape (Fig
   28). The front edges should project
   about $^1/_4$ in (6 mm).

6 Glue the dormer to the roof, making
   sure the fronts line up. Paste strips of
   cotton fabric along the join to secure
   it (Fig 29). Add $^1/_4$ in (6 mm) strip to
   form ridge.

Fig. 27 Mark position of dormer

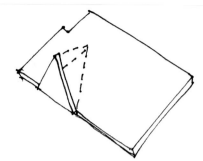

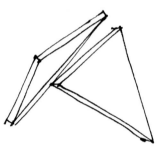

Fig. 28 Assemble dormer

Fig. 29 Tape dormer

Stone tiled roof made of strips of card, decreasing in size towards the ridge.

Roof

1 Strengthen inside the ridge of the front roof 1 in (25 mm) from the top with a beam of $^3/_8$ in (10 mm) square wood, stained light brown. Add a similar strip $^1/_2$ x $^1/_4$ in (13 x 6 mm) $^1/_4$ in (6 mm) from the bottom to support the roof on the front, cut shorter to clear the beams.

2 If you wish to leave the roof on when the front is open add support beams inside the right-hand gable and across the front of the chimney,

to act as a stop for the roof by catching the ridge pole (Fig 30).

3 Tile the roof and dormer. Cut strips of card (use cereal packets). Alternatively you can cut individual tiles of $^1/_{16}$ in (1.5 mm) ply or from thin cork sheet from a model railway shop. The rows should start 1 in (25 mm) square at the bottom, leaving $^5/_8$ in (16 mm) showing, reducing to $^3/_8$ in (10 mm) squares at the top. Cut the tiles unevenly, with a $^1/_{16}$ in (1.5 mm) gap between (Fig 31).

4 Paint the eaves and joints grey. You

can paint the tiles dark mottled grey before laying on the roof, or rely on a stiff brush for painting into the gaps after they are glued.

5 Stipple the roof with brown and olive green. It should be darker than the walls; the colour varies with moss and soot, and can look black after rain.

Some chickens and a goat can be placed outside the house, and maybe some sacks of grain and a pile of logs for the fire. If this were an Irish house, blocks of peat would be used.

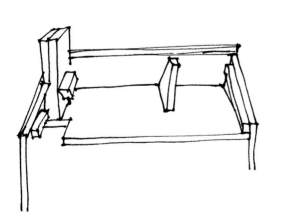
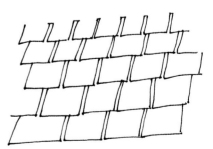

Fig. 30 Add support strips to walls and roof   *Fig. 31 Stone tiles*

CHAPTER THREE

Georgian house, 1790s

Interior of a terraced Georgian town house in 1790s. The high ceilings allow plenty of headroom below the chandeliers. The rooms are sparingly furnished, most pieces carefully arranged along the walls.

THE Georgian period (1714-1830) covers the reigns of four monarchs. The architecture varies from Baroque (Vanbrugh's Blenheim Palace and Castle Howard) and Palladian, based on sixteenth-century Italian villas and introduced to England in the seventeenth century by Inigo Jones, to the plainer neo-classical terraces of Bath, and the Regency sea-front houses in Brighton with their bow windows and cast-iron balconies.

Town houses had to be built of brick or stone. After the Great Fire of London in 1666 (graphically described in Samuel Pepys's diaries), numerous Building Acts ensured that houses were fire-resistant. Thatch had been banned from towns for two hundred years. Now wooden window frames had to be set back in the wall at least 4 in (10 cm) and wooden eaves had to be covered. This led to the building of parapets, with the roof set back behind a low wall or behind a row of stone balusters.

In a terrace the party walls extended between the roofs as a fire break. With the growing use of slates, roofs could be set at a shallower angle, and mansard roofs (a shallow angle over a steeper one) were built with dormer windows, making full use of the attics (Fig 32). The earliest chimney pots (1715) were oblong pyramid shapes, soon to be replaced by round pottery ones which were in general use by Victorian times.

Terraced housing began in Bath in the mid-eighteenth century, using the local limestone, and squares and terraces were developed in London from the 1760s in classical designs taken from ancient Greek and Roman architecture embellished with pillars and porticoes. The grand houses and country mansions were built of red brick, as were some of the Tudor and Queen Anne ones before them, but most terraces were built of white (yellow) brick, which was considered less garish en-masse. Towards the end of the century all-over rendering was introduced to simulate stone. This was self-coloured or colour washed, but the soot and smog from the coal fires blackened the houses (washable oil-based paints were not available until the 1840s).

The house shown is taken from my book Build a Doll's House, using ready-made stairs and windows. The ground floor is rusticated, with stucco (smooth cement) rendered bricks scored to resemble stonework. The floors above could be brick, but in this case they are rendered. Sometimes a colour wash was added to the plain wall, contrasting with the cream quoins and pediments.

Quoins, like alternating large stones, run down each side in imitation of the large blocks on detached houses, and a large cornice runs along the top of the facade. The tall windows on the first floor (piano nobile) have triangular pediments. The top floor ones are left plain.

You can vary the windows – look for period details on houses you see. Some have alternate curved and triangular pediments. The ground floor windows may be arched to match the doorway, with the rustication fanning outwards. Rustication always carries right up to the window opening; there is no moulded surround as seen on the other windows.

The first-floor windows, either casement or sliding sash, can start from floor level and open on to a shallow balcony which extends over the porch. Georgian windows have small panes and narrow glazing bars. They are usually sliding sashes balanced by counterweights in the window casing.

A simpler version of this house could be made without window mouldings (Fig 33), with just a flat brick wall and a straight fan of bricks for each lintel, a rusticated or just plain cream ground floor, and a ready-made front door with a square

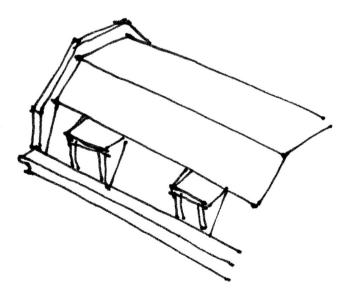

Fig. 32 Mansard roof

Fig. 33 Simple box back house

Fig. 34 Square pediment

Fig. 35 Triangular pediment

or triangular pediment (Figs 34 and 35). Sheets of moulded bricks are available in yellow or red, and their colours can be modified. A stone balcony with cast-iron railings (use wire or plastic) can run below the first-floor windows, or each can have its own balcony. A parapeted roof

should never overhang the sides; if not set between the walls, it should finish flush with them.

As the most popular doll's houses are built as six rooms on three floors with a central staircase, the design of a real house has to be adapted. Visitors to an elegant

house would not be expected to pass the kitchen – this would be hidden in the basement, or at the back of the house.

You can make a basement as a simple box with an opening front. To avoid stranding the front door in mid-air, add a triangular double

Fig. 36 Triangular double staircase

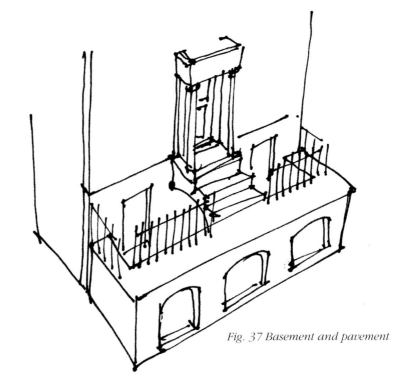

Fig. 37 Basement and pavement

staircase, like that of the Blackett doll's house in the Museum of London (Fig 36).

A raised pavement with steps down to a basement area leaves a blank panel about 6 in (15 cm) high, unless the front door is raised by at least seven steps as in the late Victorian house (see page 65). Add interest to a high pavement by cutting three arches below for coal cellars (Fig 37). If there was no room for steps to the basement, the tradesmen's entrance would have been at the back of the house. To avoid having to excavate for the basements, the main road was usually built up to the level of the front doors, the real ground level being at the back of the house. A small side road, known as a mews, gave access to stabling for the horses and carriages, and grooms' accommodation.

Most terraced houses have the staircase to one side, and are at least two rooms deep. If you are copying a real house, it is a problem deciding where it should open – back and front, or the back rooms can open each side. The six-room house shown could be adapted to a side staircase, with the rooms leading off one another (corridors were not general until Victorian times). The first floor might have double doors or be made into one large drawing room, and the library could combine with the ground floor dining room, unless you have already made more space by moving the kitchen to a basement.

Colours

Simple earth colours (dull greens and browns) were used early in the century. Prettier colours were introduced by Robert Adam in the 1760s with his white stucco

mouldings and low reliefs, a style similar to the decoration on Wedgwood pottery. It is said that cool greens and blues were used for bedrooms, warm shades of pink and red for reception rooms, and shades of yellow and cream for service areas, such as the kitchen and hallways. However, if you refer to contemporary paintings the dining room was often sage green, a bedroom could be red, and people were advised to use cool colours in a warm sunny room and pink and reds in a chilly north-facing room. Blue, green and red were all popular for reception rooms. In fact the owners must have used their own taste just as we do today.

Floors

Very grand houses had halls and pillars painted to simulate marble; even the floors could be marbled stucco. I think this is a little grandiose for a terraced town house, but black and white marble tiles look well in the hall; the large white tiles have small black ones set across the corners. This floor could be continued into the dining room, as seen in paintings of Dutch interiors, but it would be rather cold underfoot, so this one has a wooden floor.

Floorboards were left unpolished and were simply washed and rubbed with sand, as were the stairs, which left the wood very light. Sometimes, small oriental or French carpets, even Axminster, were used for warmth, particularly under the dining-room table. Otherwise the floors were often bare. A fitted carpet could be made by sewing narrow strips together – looms were too small to weave a wide carpet – and laying a rectangle, with felt or a plain carpet filling in the edges.

The entrance hall has black and white marble floor tiles

Walls

The walls could be panelled in pine, lightly varnished or painted; covered with fabric stretched or gathered on battens which could be changed summer and winter from cotton to velvet or damask; plastered and painted; or wallpapered with the oriental and French papers now being imported, or with English flocked papers. These were printed to imitate textiles – velvet, damask, figured silks, printed cottons and needlework. The pattern was applied in glue, and a fine dust of fabric shearings was sieved over the paper. In the 1760s there was a craze for a 'print room' – black and white engravings were pasted on to the wall in printed frames, like a giant scrapbook.

Woodwork

Woodwork was usually painted. Sometimes the six-panelled doors were varnished mahogany. The hall shown is painted a neutral buff, with pale wood panelling as a dado and up the stairs.

Kitchen

The kitchen could have an open wood fire, but cast-iron ranges were used in towns where coal was more available. The fire was held behind iron bars, and its width could be adjusted by movable sides (Fig 38). Pots and kettles could be swung over the fire on trivets or be kept simmering in front or on the side hobs. As there was no oven, roasting was still done in front of the fire. If the fire were wide enough, a smoke jack was still used to turn a horizontal spit, but in the late eighteenth century a clockwork bottle jack would hang the meat vertically.

Fire grates

Fire grates were needed for burning coal to keep the coal clear of the ash. The earliest ones were rectangular wrought-iron baskets with four uprights like firedogs, and were used for both cooking and heating. More elegant designs were made with polished steel bars held between brass standards, or all-steel fronts with an iron plate at the back to replace the loose fireback.

Cast-iron hob grates, with a raised fire between two flat hobs, provided a smaller version of the kitchen range and were made in the late eighteenth century with neo-classical relief patterns on the front panels. There are three shapes – the straight Pantheon grate, the semi-circular Forest grate, and the hourglass-shaped Bath grate (Figs 39-41).

Fire Surrounds

The fire surrounds or chimney-pieces were carved from marble or wood and were designed as part of the room. A panel above might hold a mirror or a painting designed to fill the space. When paintings are hung on panelled walls they must always fit within a panel and never overlap the mouldings.

Furniture

The furniture of this period was mostly made of mahogany, a hard wood which could be carved and turned. Well-known furniture makers and designers were Sheraton, Chippendale and, later, Hepplewhite. Lacquer furniture was imported from the East; the originals were black, European copies were red and green. As this house is set in the 1790s, as shown by the costumes of the inhabitants, it is too early for a sofa table, Regency dining chairs, or a Carlton house table (an elegant desk with a curved back).

Drawing room

The drawing room fireplace has a tall mirror above it. Early 'looking-glass plates' were silvered with tin foil and mercury, but it was not until the late eighteenth century that a method of spinning glass to a flat sheet about 5 ft (1.27 m) in diameter allowed large mirrors to be made. Window panes also increased in size. Larger mirrors were made by joining two panels.

If the room were larger, a console table would be placed between two windows, with a tall mirror, a pier

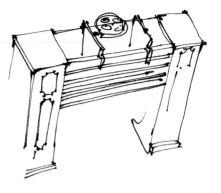

Fig. 38 Cast-iron range

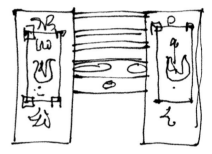

Fig. 39 Pantheon grate

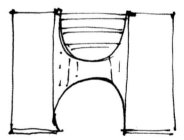

Fig. 40 Forest grate

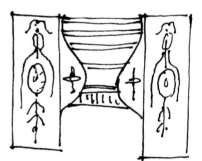

Fig. 41 Bath grate

The elegant drawing room has panels of wallpaper in rococo frames. The floor is left plain, and sanded, not polished. Furniture is set back against the walls until needed. A pet Pomeranian is allowed into the room.

glass, fixed flat on the wall above it and incorporated into the panelling (a pier being the space between two windows).

The wallpaper has charming French pastoral scenes set in rococo frames that would have been moulded in stucco. A large crystal chandelier hangs from the ceiling, reflecting more light in the mirror at night. A French ormolu clock stands on the marble chimney piece, and a pierced brass fender stops any coals falling on the floor.

A sofa and chairs are set against the walls. A tea table and a fire screen can be moved when necessary. The ladies can entertain guests on the harpsichord and harp.

Some rooms have only muslin curtains and shutters at the window. This formal room has pull-up festoon curtains and full-length split muslin curtains to keep out the sunlight.

The library has fitted bookcases, and a carpet made up from narrow strips. An elderly pug sits by grandfather's chair.

Library

The library is lined with bookshelves which are painted lime white which is used throughout the house; (brilliant white being a twentieth-century invention). A pedestal desk (two pillars of drawers, a centre drawer and flat top) stands near the window, with a comfortable leather wing chair drawn up to it. The reading lamp, known as a library lamp, on the desk has two candles in an oval shade.

A brass chandelier hangs from the ceiling and double wall sconces are positioned either side of the fire. Over the clock on the mantelpiece a painting of a horse hangs straight from two chains nailed to the cornice.

On the globe in the corner the master can follow the routes of his shipping ventures – spices from the East, fabrics from India, slaves from Africa. Chinese porcelain jars decorate the top of the bookcases. Library steps would be a spiral around a tall newel. A folding chair/steps was not made until later in Regency times. The carpet is made up from lengths of Indian or Axminster stitched together.

Houses were often let fully furnished, including the books. If a breakfront bookcase (so called because the centre section is built forward) were used instead of fitted shelves, there would be space for a bureau bookcase against the wall and a round central table, either with a plain top (a loo table after the game) or a drum table with drawers (sometimes called a rent table).

Dining room

The dining room is papered in blue damask, with a panelled white dado. These were usually white or pale in colour; it was not until Victorian times that they were darker than the wall above. Paintings of horses or ships line the room, hanging flat against the wall.

The dining chairs are arranged along the wall and only moved when a meal is served. These Chippendale chairs have the straight legs of the late 1700s. An earlier table would have been a drop-leaf with rectangular flaps that opened out, which could be extended with D-shaped or semi-circular tables at each end. By the 1750s, centre pedestals replaced the awkward legs.

A knife box on the sideboard will also contain forks. The silver tea urn is used for breakfast. There is a decorative arrangement of fruit. A wooden plate carrier (like a tub with a slot down one side) and a butler's tray, with a folding stand, are used by the maid or footman. (This is standing ready by the kitchen table)

The main meal, known as dinner, was served at about two o'clock during the early eighteenth century. By the end of the century, it was six-thirty – with luncheon filling the gap about mid-day and a light supper at about ten o'clock. All the food was laid on the table at once, and at a large dinner party a servant stood behind each chair to hand the food. Each place was laid with a knife and fork. Tablespoons for soup were laid out by the salt. The early two-pronged forks were sharp, so the food was often eaten off the rounded knife blades. The name 'table spoon' refers to their being set on the table, when previously guests were expected to bring their own eating implements. Pepys complained in 1663 that a Guildhall supper had knives only on the top two tables, and if he had not chanced to purchase a spoon he would have been forced to eat with his fingers, in which case he would have been even more aggravated by their lack of napkins. These were often folded into decorative shapes – a practice which still continues today, despite our frequent use of paper napkins.

The table was cleared and the cloth removed for the dessert and fruit. The ladies then retired to the (with-) drawing room to take tea or coffee. The gentlemen circulated the port and brandy, pushed clockwise round the table on silver coasters, and smoked their long clay pipes.

Dining room, with a two-pedestal table, and Chippendale chairs set against the walls

In the stone-flagged kitchen plates and dishes are stored on shelves along the wall. A small joint is revolving on a clockwork bottle jack in front of the fire. There is a spit rack over the mantelpiece.

Kitchen

The kitchen was often some distance from the dining room, and the food would be cold before it was served. In this house the diners are more fortunate. The food can be kept warm on the hobs and there are large tables for food preparation. Fresh food is kept in ventilated cupboards, or strung from the ceiling out of reach of vermin.

In town, the washing can be sent out to a laundry woman, and a baker will make a daily delivery. Even up to the 1940s people would pay the baker to cook for them, and he would cook everyone's turkeys on Christmas morning.

All water for washing and shaving had to be heated on the stove and carried upstairs and the dirty water carried down again. Some houses had a bath, either in its own separate room or behind a screen in a corner of the bedroom. This would be a high, wooden, oval tub, lined with tin and draped with a cloth to cover the rough edges.

Bedroom

The bedroom is painted a light blue, with the usual off-white dado. The four-poster is draped more for decoration than warmth. As it is a high bed, there are some steps at the side. Bedside tables to hold a chamber pot were not common until after 1760. Before this a chair stood beside the bed and a close-stool concealed a pottery bucket.

Copper warming pans with a hinged lid were now used, or hot embers might be placed in a wooden framework known as a bed wagon.

Dressing tables were usually draped with a cloth and a lace cover, with a mirror propped against the wall. Early eighteenth-century dressing tables had cabriole legs and a slight kneehole made by a shallow central drawer flanked by two deeper drawers. They were topped by a small swivel mirror, either on two legs or on a box base with small drawers.

Clothes were folded and stored flat in the tallboy or chest of drawers. Gentlemen's wardrobes had a short hanging cupboard to take jackets.

Nursery

The nursery is simply furnished. A diamond-patterned patchwork quilt covers the bed. There is a small mahogany corner washstand, a chest of drawers, Chippendale hanging shelves, and a side table with a writing slope concealed in the drawer. The child could have a davenport, which were made from the late 1700s. The early ones were supported on flat columns, like school desks. In the next century the desk top was supported on a column of drawers, as seen in the Victorian house on page 58. A high-backed chair, like the wall chairs in the drawing room, has a yellow-

The bedroom has a four-poster bed with silk curtains and valance, the dressing table is draped in muslin and lace

striped loose cover. A relic of early childhood is a silver rattle with a coral handle, used for teething.

Children were allowed to play instead of being treated like little adults. Georgian rocking horses had hoop rockers, small heads with an underslung jaw, and flat round eyes shaped like a chocolate penny. Hobby horses, the 'cock horse' of Banbury Cross, had a solid head on a stick, which sometimes had a wheel at the end. Ninepins, the fore-runner of American ten-pin bowling, was probably banned on Sundays in New England, so a different name was invented. Elegant wooden dolls had complete sets of clothing, and baby houses (meaning doll's houses) were made to be played

The nursery is sparsely furnished, the little girl holds a treasured wooden doll

with, unlike the Continental ones commissioned by rich collectors.

Entrance hall

The entrance hall has a console table, a mirror, and a fine mahogany grandfather clock. A plainer pine clock stands in the kitchen. Family portraits line the walls.

Lighting

Candles were the only form of lighting. The bedroom chamberstick with a wide base and a snuffer was not used as a bedside light so close to the bed hangings but was left on a piece of solid furniture. The candlesticks were taken to the kitchen every morning to be cleaned and the stubs removed from the sconces and chandeliers – so during the day it was usual to see empty wall sconces. (In the nineteenth century, Prince Albert started an economy drive by insisting that the candles at Windsor were burnt to the end, instead of being left as perks for the servants.) The lighted candlesticks and candelabra were brought into the reception rooms as darkness fell and the shutters or curtains were closed. Candlesticks were left ready in the hall, which is lit by a candle lantern, to be carried up to the bedrooms. They were lit from the fire by a taper or a spill of curled wood shaving.

The family

The family living in this house are dressed in the style of the 1790s, before trousers replaced breeches in Regency times, and later than the fashion for powdered hair and wigs. The ladies wear large hats, with gathered scarves modestly covering their square necklines, just like Gainsborough portraits.

The Georgian style was still used for liveried servants in the next century. Footmen wore knee breeches, stockings and buckled shoes. Mrs Beeton describes how they should set their hair in rolls with flour and water!

MAKING AND DECORATING THE HOUSE

The colour schemes and furniture shown will suit any large Georgian house. The rooms are 12 in (30.5 cm) wide by 16 in (40.6 cm) deep. The heights are 9 $\frac{3}{8}$ in (23.8 cm), 11 $\frac{1}{4}$ in (28.6 cm) and 10 $\frac{1}{4}$ in (26 cm). Anything smaller would be rather cramped.

Decide on your own colour scheme, but remember to choose the wall colours and period papers to tone with each other and any upholstered furniture you may already have. As the exterior is a fairly dark cream, I have used tones of blue and a deep pink. A lighter pink might clash.

You will need:

- large six-room doll's house approx 33 in wide by 15 in deep (84 x 38 cm) or kit or Build a Doll's House and two 8 x 4 ft (2.44 x 1.22 m) sheets of $\frac{3}{8}$ in (10 mm) ply or MDF, windows, stairs, assorted strip woods and mouldings for exterior
- white emulsion or acrylic primer
- emulsion paint sample pots: lime white, old white, drab, porphyr pink, off-black
- cream paint (Farrow & Ball satin)
- Terre Vert (turquoise) (sample Fired Earth)
- wood flooring, natural
- moulded panels for staircase and hall

- six-panelled doors
- cornice and skirting, picture rail
- small mitre block and saw
- card for dado panelling, small dado rail and small moulding
- Stanley or craft knife
- metal ruler or straight edge
- self-heal cutting mat
- stair carpet or braid, and brown card (for library carpet)
- $\frac{3}{8}$ in (10 mm) panels (for chimney breasts)
- 5 fireplaces and grates or fire baskets
- wood for kitchen fire surround
- cast-iron range, or fittings for an open fire

- stone flag flooring (optional)
- black and white tile paper (for hall)
- wooden internal shutters
- fine cotton muslin and raw silk (for curtains)
- fine chains, gold thread and small brass pins (for hanging pictures)
- bradawl
- pin punch
- small pliers
- small hammer
- wallpapers and wallpaper paste
- brushes and paint roller
- clear glue, white wood glue, fabric glue

CONSTRUCTION

1 For a smooth finish paint the panels before assembling, if possible. Use a smooth roller, and paint the front before adding any mouldings. (If using a small pot apply the paint to the roller with a brush.) If decorating an assembled house, use a 1 in (2.5 cm) soft brush and protect the wood floors with masking tape and card or plastic. Do not paint the floors apart from the hall, which will be papered, and the kitchen if you wish to paint flagstones. Wood flooring and moulded flagstones can be applied later, or floorboards drawn in now, about $^3/_4$ in (19 mm) apart, and coloured with a light wash of diluted wood stain – do not varnish.

2 White emulsion or acrylic primer can be used as a base. Walls and ceilings to be lime white can be painted directly, as can the old white in the kitchen, which should also be distressed to look sooty. Acrylic primer has an oily finish that will not take thin washes of 'soot'.

3 Undercoat coloured and papered walls. Mask adjacent walls with masking tape and roll several thin coats of coloured emulsion until smooth, allowing some hours between each coat. Make sure a painted surface is quite dry before using masking tape on it. Wallpaper the house after assembly. Decorate the inside front later to match the rooms (the panels measured from ceiling to ceiling, with no mouldings).

4 Cut chimney breasts (if needed) from $^3/_8$ in (10 mm) ply or MDF, or build up deeper ones with strip wood if necessary for the grates or fire baskets. They should be about 1 in (2.5 cm) wider than the fireplace. Cut a hole to fit the opening. Paint to match the room, and paint the inside of the opening black.

5 Before assembling check the doors will fit their openings, and that the library door will open over the carpet, which will be pasted on to card.

6 If using kit stairs, try them against the hall walls to check where to cut them, and the depth of the landings. A kit with separate treads already drilled for the banisters is easiest to use. You may need to cut the top step into the landing for the newels to line up (Fig 42), or simply add a strip to the half landings for the return stairs to rest on (Fig 43).

7 Tack the house together lightly and check that the front fits. If the box is slightly out of square, or is wider than the front, take it apart and file or sand the back to fit. In final assembly do not force the floors. If they are too tight they can push the sides out. Do not finish the front until the house is assembled in case a final adjustment needs a strip down one side, which can be hidden by the quoins and rustication. Wallpaper, add hall tiles, and fit the stairs. Finish the interior before hanging the front.

8 Assemble the front, except for the porch, before hanging on a piano hinge. Mark the screw holes and try on two screws. If you make a mistake, you can turn the hinge upside down and make new screw holes.

Stairs

1 It is easiest to fit flights assembled separately, with newels on the top and bottom steps. These will be different heights on the landings. Many doll's houses are supplied like this – you must decide if the gap between is safe or add a handrail that joins either at an angle, or on a turned section of the newel.

2 If the gap needs banisters they will need to be raised on a base strip (Fig 44). The top landing does not need

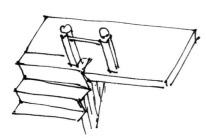

Fig. 42 Cut stairs into landing

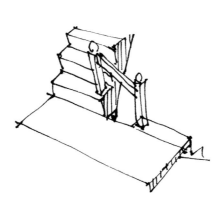

Fig. 43 Butt up stairs to landing

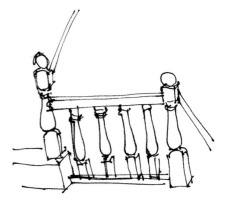

Fig. 44 Landing banisters

Fig. 45 Extend landing

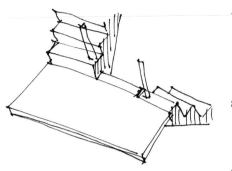

its own newels, but can run from the top newel to the wall.

3 You can butt up both flights to the landing (Fig 45) and extend the landing between them. The underneath of the bottom step should be trimmed flush. Alternatively the bottom newels can be fixed to the landings (Fig 42).

4 If the treads are not pre-drilled, mark $\frac{1}{8}$ in (3 mm) from the edge centred on each tread. Some banisters have a small point on the bottom which will need a locating hole to be made with a bradawl.

5 Use a clear glue (i.e. Bostik or Uhu) so that the banisters are not rigid.

6 Try the handrail over the banisters and hold the newels behind it to find their position (Fig 46). Drill, pin (use a length of paper clip, cut with the

Fig. 46 Position newel posts

side cutter on the pliers) and glue the newels with wood glue.

7 When the newels are firm, cut the handrail to fit and glue over the banisters with wood glue on the top of each. Push them firmly upright against the handrail so that all are parallel.

8 The stairs should be lightly stained to look like mature wood and distressed in the corners. Dilute wood stain with white spirit.

9 Once the house is firmly pinned and glued or screwed and the floors are in place, you can fix the front landings, adding wood flooring or marking to match the floors. If they are a tight fit, you can hammer them in place using a piece of scrap wood to protect the edge you hit. Glue the wall not the landing to avoid smearing the wall. You can prop the landings on spacers cut to height from scrap wood or support them on a small cornice glued beforehand (essential if the landing is not a tight fit).

10 Check the bottom flights against each back landing before fixing it, extending where necessary. Then fix the top half landing.

11 Glue the stairs in place. They will need supporting until dry, or holding underneath the landings with masking tape. Do not tape to the walls as this could mark them.

12 Add the dado after the doors are hung. Moulded panels are available, angled for a left- or right-hand wall. The colour can be changed and distressed to match the wooden stairs. Paint the wall by the treads too.

Flooring

Lay sheets of wood flooring before fitting the chimney breasts and skirting. Check the doors will open over them.

Doors

The doors should be six-panelled for a Georgian house, four-panelled for Victorian.

1 Rehang three doors, so they will open with their backs to the room. Remove the bottom pin, or break the frame and rehang on the other side, with the top pin fixed, the other retractable. Cut a length of wire paper clip, and drill a hole its full length into the door. Hold the pin in place with a knife blade until it can

The stairs are plain wood with natural wood panelling.

drop into a hole in the frame – remember to seal with a strip of sellotape underneath or it will fall straight through! Once in the house it will be secure. When doors are damaged you can replace the pin in the same way.

2   Paint or varnish all doors. Those on the first floor are stained and varnished. The architrave and skirting in the drawing room are painted pink, as the lime white used elsewhere would clash with the background colour. The doors cannot be fitted until the walls are decorated.

Fireplaces

Glue the chimney breasts after checking that the fireplaces (chimney pieces) fit. The hearthstone in front should fit within the fender (if any), and can be glued under the chimney breast. Use dark grey or marbled paper. Paint the recess black.

Bedrooms

1   Fix a white chair rail in the two bedrooms, using a 3 in (7.6 cm) high strip of card as a guide. The moulding is wider at the top (the reverse of skirting). Mitre into the corners and butt up to the fireplaces.

2   Glue the skirting and a small cornice (if wiring add later) and fix the doors.

3   The wall colour is continued on the

inside front of the house to complete the colour scheme when the curtains are hung, but mouldings are not necessary as they have to be cut well clear of the walls and floors. These panels of paint and paper butt up at ceiling level.

Drawing room

1   The drawing room is papered with the background colour supplied with the panels, cut just short of the top and bottom to allow for gluing the cornice and skirting to the wood.

2   The left-hand wall is papered in two pieces, joining on the far side of the chimney breast. An $1/8$ in (3 mm) overlap continues on to the back wall from both sides. Use a sharp craft or Stanley knife and metal ruler on a self-heal rubber mat when cutting the paper. A raised, sort of corrugated ruler is safest to use to avoid cutting your fingers.

3   Paint the wallpaper paste on the side walls and paper. Position, and press from the centre with a soft cloth, working outwards to expel the excess paste. Wait until this has dried flat before papering the back wall. Cut the paper from the doorway. (If you have wired your house with single copper tape, you need to use a special paste without fungicide (or varnish the tape) to stop corrosion.)

4   Glue the door, skirting and cornice before positioning the panels. As there is no chair rail you can use a skirting that has an extra moulding at the bottom to keep chair legs away from the wall. Trim the panels close to the 'mouldings'. Lay them on the floor to check the spacing – if they are more than $1/2$ in (13 mm) apart they will not look like panels. This pattern used two wide, one medium, and two thin panels on the back wall, two wide, one medium, and one thin on the right-hand wall, plus part of a medium panel above the door, two wide panels on the left hand wall. The front will need a medium and a wide panel. Check the space left around the curtain.

5   Cut a strip of card to line up the bottom edges, or even a second strip of skirting wedged in place. Mark the spaces on it as a guide, and paste the panels. You will need to wipe any surplus paste from the background afterwards.

6   Make a $5 1/2 \times 3 1/2$ in (14 x 9 cm) mirror from mirror card and a 1/4 in (6 mm) gold frame. If you wish to make a taller mirror, it should have a join in the glass at 5 or $5 1/2$ in (13 or 14 cm) high.

7   Glue hearth, fireplace and mirror.

8   Fix a ceiling rose and hook to the ceiling for the chandelier. If wiring the house, run the wire through the back wall before fitting the cornice.

9   Cut a curtain of deep pink raw silk the height of the window and 2 in (5 cm) wider than it. Turn the edges

with fabric glue or invisible thread. You can fringe the bottom edge by pulling out the cross threads. Run a gathering thread along the top edge. To pull up into two festoons, fold the fabric into $^3/_8$ in (10 mm) pleats, run threads up the sides and centre, and pull up like a Venetian blind. Gather the top to fit the window and arrange the festoons (Fig 47). Glue to the inside of a shaped pelmet or arrange over a $^1/_2$ in (12 mm) batten. Fine muslin curtains are hung behind on a dowel or metal rod. They can be soaked in wallpaper paste or starch to hang straight, and trimmed at floor level. Use a little fabric glue along the bottom to prevent fraying. Similar curtains can be made from cream silk and muslin for the bedroom.

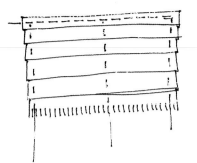
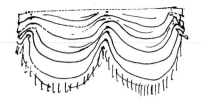

Fig. 47 Pull up curtain

Library

1   Cut brown mounting card to fit the floor. Try the bookshelves in place and cut strips of stair carpet to fit up to them, and clear of the fireplace. Glue with fabric glue. Wood glue the card to the floor, making sure the door will open; it may need sanding.

2   The bookshelves are made from mass-produced shelving – one of three cupboards, two of two cupboards, and two singles cut down to fit the corners. The mouldings are cut back to fit in the left-hand corner,

and the top is filled in. The lime white needs distressing with a thin colour or wood stain to show up the mouldings. A deep pink makes a warm background colour without being too dark. Fill the shelves with cheap mass-produced books, blocks of books, printed and photographic spines, or make your own sets of volumes by scoring blocks of wood, covering with leather and marking with gold leaf.

3   The dado matches the height of the cupboards. Cut some smooth art card in panels to fit around the walls and fireplace. Add skirting and a chair rail mitred in the corners. Paint, glue and fit the door.

4   Fix the fireplace. There may be no room for a projecting hearth. If the fire basket does not protrude, use a flat fender.

5   Hang the central brass chandelier and fix wall sconces on either side of the fire. These may be fixed on brass pins, fitting them into a recess on the back with some grip-wax or Bostik. Hang a horse painting or seascape over the fire on fine gold chains, gold twine or brass wire. The painting should hang flat: it would have had rings in the top of the frame. Use fine brass pins to fix the chain to the cornice. If the whole wall is panelled some pictures may be painted to fit exactly within a panel. They must never extend

across mouldings.

6   Split curtains of fine muslin are hung on a brass rod (you can buy extending ones, or glue brass doorknobs or beads on to a brass tube), held on small screw eyes. Wooden shutters are shorter than the window, to allow some light in when closed in daytime. These are glued flat on the wall; they would really be folded into the wall of the window recess.

Dining room

1   Cut the damask pattern carefully to centre on the back wall and match at the corners.

2   The right-hand wall can be papered in one strip if you start carefully at the back and press it firmly into the back corner of the chimney breast and tight round to the front.

3   The dado is made from thick white card as before, but to full 3 in (7.5 cm) height. It can be plain, but the

more important the room the more panelling it had. Cut the back panel to fit right across, with the sides butted up not mitred. The back skirting and chair rail are mitred but not glued yet. With them wedged in place cut the side mouldings to fit.

4 With a soft pencil, sketch in where the panels could fit – $^1/_4$ in (6 mm) space top and bottom, $^3/_8$ in (10 mm) in between, and 3-3 $^1/_4$ in (7.6-8.3 cm) long. When they look correct, rule accurate guide lines. You can have a lot of fun mitring small rounded mouldings to fit!

5 Glue and fix the mouldings, then paint the dado and cornice lime white before fixing in place with the door and the fireplace.

6 You can hang a crystal chandelier, or light the table with a pair of silver candelabra. Silver wall sconces can be fixed over the sideboard.

7 An elegant gilt mirror is hung over the fire on an inconspicuous brass pin.

8 Oil paintings are hung from the picture rail just below the cornice, on small hooks or nails. Glue a long loop of gold thread to the back of each picture with paper patches, making it just long enough to hang straight from one nail, run along the cornice, and back down from a

second nail (as if the picture is hung on two chains).

9 Split curtains of muslin are hung on the the remaining windows, including the staircase, and shutters are used on the ground floor for security.

Kitchen

The fire surround is 5 in (12.7 cm) wide by 5 $^1/_2$ in (14 cm) high, to fit the open range. The chimney above has been made of 1 in (2.5 cm) balsa. Paint old white to match the walls, and distress the room with diluted black dabbed on with a sponge, or real soot or charcoal rubbed in, particularly over the fire. The back of the fireplace would be black in the centre, above the fire.

Cut the moulded flagstones to fit round the fireplace (if not already painted on the floor). They can be re-painted in several shades of stone, using black, white and yellow ochre.

A spit rack above the mantelpiece may not be needed now a clockwork bottle jack is used, but is a relic of earlier cooking. Storage shelves run along two walls, $^7/_8$ in (22 mm) wide, supported on wooden brackets. These are used for serving dishes and wooden storage bins. Other food is kept in the wire-fronted cupboard, or in spice drawers hung on the wall. Sacks of food will be hung clear of the floor when not in use.

Furnishing

Some of this furniture is handmade, but many pieces are mass-produced. The four-poster bed has been draped in silk to match the curtains, with a pleated pelmet and valance, and 'embroidered' coverlet made from strips of stair carpet. The wall chairs have been painted pink. Another, in the nursery, has a slip cover of yellow-striped seersucker as yellow check was unavailable.

CHAPTER FOUR

Victorian house, 1870s

Interior of a terraced Victorian house of 1870s, lit by oil lamps and candles.
The large rooms allow space for a realistic arrangement of furniture, often very cluttered at this period.

QUEEN Victoria reigned from 1837 to 1901, and during her long reign Britain prospered. The Great Exhibition of 1851 was intended to show the ultimate in world-wide design of furniture and manufactured goods. This was the time of the Industrial Revolution, the invention of the steam engine, for running machinery as well as transporting goods and passengers. Many poor families who had lost their livelihood with the enclosure of land to create parks for the landowners had drifted to the towns, their wretched lives are described in Dickens' novels

Other people profited from the new wealth, from trade and overseas commerce, creating a growing middle-class who could afford large town houses and a villa in the country. I have furnished the comfortable terraced brick house shown for a well-to-do family of the 1870s. The bay windows are typical of later Victorian houses. The developments of the 1840s were still of Georgian designs, so you could also furnish the previous house in Victorian style.

A flat-fronted house can be adapted. When cutting openings for the bays, either keep the original wall below the window to make a deep window sill, or cut a little lower to make a window seat. If you continue the floor into the bay it will give more space, which is very useful for a table and aspidistra, or other clutter (Fig 48).

If you build up the bays from thin $^1/_8$ in (3 mm) wood, there will be fewer problems with cutting an angle. Mass-produced and British bay windows are available. The roof on the imported version goes to a point, which should be altered to one rectangular panel and two triangles (Fig 49), or the front panel angled straight back from the corner when viewed straight on (Fig 50). The sills should continue round the bay, separating the windows from the brick wall.

Some Victorian houses were still rendered in stucco, but it proved expensive to maintain as it needed repainting every five years and repairing when damaged by frost and rain water. Brickwork needed very little maintenance.

The house shown (which is 39 in wide by 15 in deep (99 x 38 cm)) is of brick, with stone or stucco lintels, parapet and window sills. The sliding sash windows have two large panes, but could have just one pane top and bottom. You can paint the brickwork (use a cream base with a thin mottled red scratched through to indicate mortar) or use sheets of

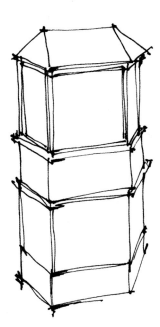

Fig. 49 Square bay roof

Fig. 50 Angled bay roof

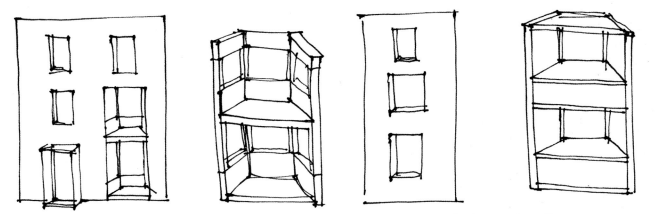

Fig. 48 Cut opening for bay to floor level or cut smaller openings for deep window sills

pre-formed coloured bricks glued on with wood glue – other glues might react with the material.

The bricks are continued round the chimneys. Painted doll's houses conventionally have the chimneys the same colour as the side wall (as seen on the Georgian house), although they would really be brick. They also look better on the gable ends of the house, even if the fireplaces are on the back wall (as is often found in antique doll's houses). Another convention is that the kitchen is usually on the bottom left.

The slate roof would be finished with black pottery ridge tiles moulded to a V-shape.

The front door is set back in a 1 in (2.5 cm) porch. The brick arch is formed with fan of 'rubbed' bricks – they were rubbed to a wedge shape to fit the curve. Fortunately we can just use scissors! You can add decorative 'stucco' mouldings; study the variety of doorways on Victorian houses.

Lighting

Oil lighting was now generally used, and, after 1860 with the invention of paraffin, it was less smelly. The hall was usually lit by a hanging lantern light. Candles and oil lamps were carried to light the way upstairs, while the staircase and corridors were left unlit.

In the reception rooms oil lamps were hung from the ceiling, on the wall, in wrought-iron standards, and on tables. The clear glass chimney was often shielded with a translucent glass shade, white or coloured, and sometimes very decoratively moulded. To subdue the light in gloomy Victorian rooms they were even draped in gathered and fringed cottons and silks, which must have been highly inflammable.

Fig. 51 Gathered lampshade

Make a shade by fringing the bottom edge of some fine cotton, then gathering it by drawing some threads near the top (Fig 51). It can fit over a Tiffany shade.

Candles were still used for the dining room – they were thought to give a more flattering light. Oil lamps and candlesticks were used in the bedroom and could easily be re-lit now that matches were available. Lamps had to be re-filled and the wicks trimmed by the servants each morning. Safe night lights were made for the nursery, shaped like oil cans and filled with wadding which soaked up the paraffin and could not spill.

Heating

Most rooms, even the servants', had fireplaces. High fireguards were hooked on to the nursery fire surround to protect the children. The fireplace was once again the focal point of the room, and the mantelpiece was decorated with mirrors, ornaments, and clocks, and often had a draped pelmet to match the curtains. The chimney flues were usually built into thick walls, leaving the fireplace flat against the wall. Fire openings were enclosed by grates, to reduce smoke. Small hob grates were still popular for bedrooms, but the arched grate surround was in general

use from the 1860s. Register doors, or movable iron plates, were fitted above the grate to regulate the draught and control the fire. Fortunately these stopped the use of small boys for cleaning chimneys – some as narrow as 9 x 14 in (22 x 35 cm) – and sweeps began to use extending brushes. They referred to chimneys as four-rod, six-rod, etc., depending on how many rods had to be screwed together to reach the top.

The fire surrounds were usually made of marble, black marble or polished slate in the dining room, and wood in the bedrooms.

Nursery

The children spent most of their time in the nursery, being brought downstairs for half an hour's inspection by their parents at teatime or when visitors were present. Their life, and diet, were ruled by the nanny or the governess. If there were space, there was a day nursery for playing and learning and a night nursery for sleeping. Boys and girls were separated at an early age. Until the twentieth century, little boys were dressed in skirts until the age of five, or even seven, and there was a great ceremony when they were 'breeched' and their curls cut off.

The nursery could be rather bleak as it was not on general view, with plain blue or green walls (supposedly to avoid eye strain). The children wrote on slates and read 'improving' books. They were taught to stand up straight with back-boards and by balancing books on their heads.

Sunday was a day for church going. My great-aunt, born in 1890, said they used to spend the whole day walking the five miles to and from church for the various services. No play was permitted on Sunday, and certainly no cards. A Noah's ark was allowed as a Sunday toy, and the only books the Bible and Pilgrim's Progress.

There might be a rocking horse (the safety rocker was patented in 1880; previously they were on hoops), a doll's house, pull-along wooden toys, alphabet bricks, bagatelle, wooden or wax dolls, and a sampler stitched by the little girl of the house. Books varied from Edward Lear's Nonsense Alphabet to Robert Louis Stephenson's Treasure Island, and there were picture books of nursery rhymes.

Plain split curtains hang either side of the window on a cornice pole, and thin muslin ones keep out the sun. The floorboards are left plain, and frequently scrubbed. A loose rug might sometimes be used.

The bed, mirror chest and washstand are painted a distressed cream. A hip bath and towel horse stand in the corner behind a folding scrap screen. The table has a paisley cloth, covered at mealtimes with a white cloth. The balloon back chairs have 'horsehair' seats (coloured with black felt-tip pen). The typical Victorian bow-fronted chest of drawers could have flat wooden handles added. A chintz covered chair would be used by the nanny or governess.

Bedroom

The bedroom has a half-tester bed, adapted from the earlier four-posters which were now considered stuffy, although these were still used in old-fashioned houses and inns (as described by Charles Dickens in the exploits of Mr Pickwick).

It was fashionable to match the drapes to the curtains and even the chair covers. Cotton slip covers were often used, even in the main rooms, to protect upholstery or for summer use, alternating with heavier covers in the winter. Pictures of Queen Victoria's bedroom at Osborne on the Isle of Wight, and of her sitting room in Buckingham Palace, show very cosy chintz covered armchairs and sofas. Furniture was not yet made in three-piece suites, but upholstered furniture could be unified by the same loose covers. Most rooms had fitted carpets, and the Queen's love of tartan at Balmoral was widely copied.

The nursery has plain walls and simple furniture. The balloon back chairs are upholstered with horsehair.

The half-tester bed is draped to match the bedroom wallpaper and curtains, the tartan carpet is similar to that used by Queen Victoria at Balmoral in Scotland

The washstand would have a tiled or marble top and splash back. (You can add marble paper to a wooden one.) The maid would bring hot water from the kitchen, and add cold water from the jug already there. Soap was now manufactured.

Matching washstand sets of ewer, basin, soap dish, slop bucket and chamber pot were made in a variety of designs. Instead of the 'close stool' a chamber pot was usually kept discreetly in a closed bedside cupboard, or there was a wooden commode with a lidded china bucket (the name comes from their being originally disguised as a chest of drawers, a French 'commode'). Hip baths were made

of tin or papier mâché and painted cream inside and a dark cream or brown outside. You had to sit in it with your feet on the floor while a maid or valet poured a jug of hot water over you.

Framework folding screens were covered with gathered fabric (Fig 52). Solid panels were covered in scraps or prints. In a reception room they were often covered in embossed and gilded leather, or were hand-painted with oriental patterns of flowers and birds.

There is a full-length wardrobe, a dressing table with a swing mirror, a cheval mirror, and a small writing desk, or davenport, with a letter rack of papier mâché. Some silhouettes have been improved with black card frames.

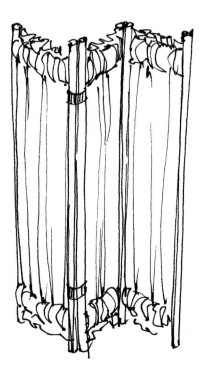

Fig. 52 Gathered screen

Drawing room

The drawing room was always feminine, and lighter than the more masculine dining room. The wallpaper chosen looks very authentic and covers the whole wall. The fireplace has a large overmantel mirror.

An oil chandelier with white glass shades is suspended from a ceiling rose. Additional light for reading comes from table lamps and candles.

As there is no study, a tall Georgian bureau bookcase has been included; a contemporary roll-top desk would be too heavy and quite out of place. Instead of the furniture being set around the walls and moved when necessary, the Victorians arranged theirs in companionable groups. There was usually a round table in the centre of the room covered in a coloured or patterned cloth with a book laid on it – no one read a book on their knee. When tea was brought in, the table was covered with a white cloth.

Often smaller tables have chairs grouped around them, for taking tea, or playing cards or chess.

Upholstered furniture now has springing and is deeply buttoned to control the padding. It is covered in damask, velvet or horsehair; leather is reserved for the study or the dining room. Antimacassars are used on the chair backs to protect them from gentlemen's hair oil. A buttonback sofa and chair have been coloured a deep green with a felt-tip pen. There are fire screens and foot stools, nesting tables and a corner what-not (a three-tier table).

Victorian rooms seem cluttered but they had a definite pathway through the furniture. Every surface is

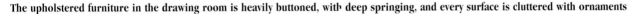

The upholstered furniture in the drawing room is heavily buttoned, with deep springing, and every surface is cluttered with ornaments

The music room can be used for recitals, dancing or card games, the club fender adds further seating.

Fig. 53 Draped curtain with tails

covered with a variety of ornaments, photographs, pictures, books, potted plants or cushions. Paintings line the walls. They could be family watercolours, landscapes and studies brought back from cultural tours of Italy, but this room has a good selection of oil paintings. Sentimental subjects were popular.

A diamond-patterned fitted carpet covers the floor, with a deep pink oriental carpet in the centre. Heavily draped curtains cover most of the window, and thick lace curtains hung inside the bay cut out much of the light. There would have been a layer of muslin before the lace, and probably a roller blind. Hang the lace curtains in the window by gluing at the top. (These are a fine self-patterned cotton, as most lace

looked too coarse against the fine detail of the wallpaper.) The main curtains can be looped up at the sides; when drawn they would trail on the ground. The pelmet is draped over a pole, and can have tails arranged in folds at the sides (Fig 53). These can be made separately.

Either fringe the edge of the draped pelmet or sew fine braid to it. Cut the long curtains to length, allowing for the drape. Turn the top to allow for a 1/8 in (3 mm) dowel or brass rod to be pushed through. If the curtains are to stay in formal folds they will need to be soaked in starch (spray starch will do) or thin wallpaper paste, then arranged in folds on their rods and left to dry before being fixed in screw-eyes on either side of the window. Glue a doorknob or similar to each end of the rods to stop them from falling out of the eyes.

Music room

A grand piano in the music room is used for recitals, solo performances, or for accompanying a singer. If the guests wish to dance (maybe to a Strauss waltz), the carpet can be rolled up to leave a smooth parquet, or linoleum, floor. (Use paper parquet stained mahogany.)

The patterned green dado and matching striped wallpaper make a good background for the black piano. There is a Canterbury to hold the sheet music, and a club fender gives extra seating and protects the dancers' skirts from the fire. A few

delicate chairs are set around the room and by the card table. A selection of seascapes hang slightly away from the walls on single hooks.

The curtains can be draped similarly to those in the drawing room, or as simple tie-backs on a pole (Fig 54).

Kitchen

The kitchen has a (paper) stone-flagged floor, and whitewashed, slightly smoke-grimed walls. No skirting is necessary on a stone floor as it would rot with the damp. The cast-iron kitchen range has a closed hob top, an oven and a water tank. Water is heated on the hot plates and the irons are set there to heat. A

Fig. 54 Tie-backs on pole

The cook is preparing the second course. The parlour maid has announced dinner and will be required to hand the dishes round the table. The scullery maid does all the rough work

The hall is lit by a hanging candle lantern.

kitchen dresser was sometimes built in right across the shorter wall, facing the fire. The dresser's base might contain cupboards, or even be used as a chicken coop with slatted bars.

This kitchen has a large 7 ft (2 m) dresser painted a dull green on the back wall. It is used for storage jars and meat platters. Bowls and crocks are stored in the cupboard underneath and on the high shelves. Pottery is replacing wood for the storage of bread and flour.

Due to the lack of space in a doll's house, the sink, with its plate rack, and the wringer are also in the kitchen instead of being in a scullery and a wash house. Steel knives used to rust, and are cleaned in the circular knife cleaner against rotating strips of leather.

A large well-scrubbed table is used for food preparation, ironing, and the servants' meals. The cook would have a comfortable wooden armchair with stools or benches for other staff. The maid cleans the house, makes the beds, and serves at the table.

Hall

The hall is tiled with black and white 'marble' tiles (a glossy plastic sheet), with a border around the edge. The stairs are stained and varnished, with a string course (skirting) along the side wall. The Turkey carpet is held with brass stair rods ($1/16$ in (1.5mm) brass rod glued in place). The wallpaper is a floral design, with a 3 in (7.6 cm) dado of anaglypta paper, coloured with a brown wash and dark-brown shoe polish. Family portraits hang on the walls. There is a

The first course is laid ready on the dining table. The new form of serving a la russe would have meant serving from the side table, with only the flowers, glass and dessert on the table.

The skirt is gathered up into a bustle

The gentleman wears a frock coat

silver wine cooler and two glass decanters in a tantalus (a carrying frame with a lock).

The sturdy table has carved cabriole legs, but it is always covered by a protective coloured cloth, usually of green baize. To keep the white cloth (a fine cotton handkerchief) in place it was sprayed with starch and wrapped in cling film until dry. The dining chairs are a Victorian copy of a popular late seventeenth-century design, in keeping with the Gothic clock on the mantelpiece. The room doubles as a library, with a large bookcase along one wall.

The walls are hung with sporting pictures of horses and fish, and there are two stuffed fish in cases. Thick red curtains (they would be velvet) hang on a brass cornice pole.

barometer, a shell-backed hall chair, painted dark brown and polished, and a marble-topped hall stand with a silver salver for visiting cards.

Dining Room

Red and green were popular colours for dining rooms. The red damask wallpaper sets off the white cloth and the silver, and the dado is painted a matching red. The Turkish carpet has a surround of green (velvet glued over the whole floor). The table is laid for dinner, with a soup tureen, and maybe a fish dish – see Mrs Beeton's cookery book for authentic table plans. A cranberry glass epergne holds a small flower arrangement. The dessert is ready on a side table, but three more hot courses will be laid on the table first. On the sideboard stand a tea urn, a

Costume

The ladies are dressed in 1870s style, with skirts looped up at the back in a bustle and flat hats. Once they were married, or considered spinsters, they all wore lace bonnets or a confection of ribbons. Visitors kept their hats on indoors.

Fashions changed considerably during Queen Victoria's reign. In the 1840s there were bonnets, sloping shoulders, tight V-waisted bodices and bell-shaped skirts. In the 1850s the bonnets were smaller, with the brim and crown as one. By the 1860s hats replaced bonnets and crinolines replaced the layers of petticoats for holding out skirts – a frame of whalebone ballooned out the skirt at the back, making the wearer glide along like a ship in full sail.

Men's fashions changed little. Knee-length frock coats, seamed at the waist, were worn indoors and out. Morning coats were cut away at

the waist, then curved towards the back. Shorter jackets were curved at the front and not waisted.

The servants wore gathered mob caps. The parlour maid wore a coloured or print dress in the morning, changing to black in the afternoon. (From this we can tell that the meal shown is taking place at mid-day and not in the evening.)

Sailor suits were popular for children from the 1860s to the 1920s, with white in summer and navy in winter. Sometimes they wore velvet suits with lace collars. Girls were dressed like their mothers, but with short, frilled skirts and visible lace-trimmed drawers. The Kate Greenaway illustrations of the 1880s were of a romantic, nostalgic style, popular with the artists of the Aesthetic Movement. Bonnets in these illustrations were from a much earlier period.

CHAPTER FIVE

Late Victorian house, 1890s

Interior of a less prosperous late Victorian house with a basement kitchen and bathroom plumbing, lit throughout by gas and oil lamp

THIS smaller terraced house has a basement, or semi-basement, as the ground floor is raised by seven steps, so some light reaches the kitchen. The decorating scheme can be adapted for any Victorian house, preferably with a bay window.

The house is built of dark, or weathered, red brick. The cream-coloured mouldings around the door, lintels, window sills and window surrounds may be stone, or cement rendering (stucco) painted with an oil-based paint. The brick edges of the window openings may be painted or left plain brick. The basement wall is rendered and painted cream, partly to lighten the area but also to help weatherproof the brick. The front steps are white, and are rubbed every morning with hearthstone, a sort of hard chalk, by the maid. The pavement and the basement area are paved with flagstones. Cast-iron railings line the steps and the pavement.

Servants and tradesmen use the basement entrance. The milkman calls several times a day: before breakfast, then before lunch with more milk and cream. The baker and butcher call to take orders from the cook or the mistress to be delivered later in the day. The fishmonger calls every Friday. This custom continues today now there are fewer fishmonger shops, particularly in country areas.

Once inside the front door, which is usually painted dark blue, Brunswick green, or wood-grained, there is a dark narrow hall with encaustic floor tiles (they are multicoloured and usually geometric in pattern, the colour fired in during manufacture).

Match boarding, tongue-and-grooved 6 in (15 cm) panelling protects the lower part of the wall and hides any rising damp. As there is a basement this should not be a problem on the ground floor, but it is essential below ground level.

Lighting

The house is lit by coal gas. This was the most popular form of lighting from the 1870s until the early 1900s, when electric lighting took over (having been available from the 1880s). After 1900 gas was widely used for cooking and heating, being cleaner and more labour-saving than coal.

Floors

Towards the end of the nineteenth century, houses were still cluttered. Fitted carpets were considered unhygienic; it was recommended that a rectangular carpet, not cut away to fit round alcoves and fireplaces, should be at least 2 ft (61 cm) away from the walls, and the surrounding floorboards be stained or varnished instead of being covered with an infill of felt, plain carpet or even linoleum. (It is interesting that during the last couple of decades, modern houses have had to cope with infestations of fleas and cockroaches, which thrive on fitted carpets and central heating!)

Bedroom

Bedroom floors were regularly scrubbed, so the loose rugs were easily removed. After any infectious disease, such as scarlet fever, the room was fumigated with sulphur smoke by a specialist, rather as we now deal with woodworm, and all the soft furnishings, as well as the children's soft toys and books, were burnt.

Brass and iron bedsteads replaced the draped half-testers and valances no longer swept the floor. In her book of Household Management, Mrs Beeton was rather ahead of her time in recommending in the 1860s that the bedroom windows should be left open for at least an hour to air the room and the bedclothes pulled clear of the bed. The heavily-draped windows, with their enveloping layers of net and lace, would have been difficult to open.

Wallpapers

William Morris wallpapers were popular, with their formal designs of birds and flowers based on the flat patterns of medieval designs. From the 1860s his studio designed furniture, fabrics and paper, and started the Arts and Crafts Movement. Many of his friends were pre-Raphaelites painters; Millais, Rossetti and Burne-Jones all harked back to romantic ideals.

The wallpapers used in the hall and parlour are William Morris, but not the stridently obvious ones. The subtle colours and patterns would have fitted into most households at the end of the century, and the revival of interest in the 1960s encouraged Liberty, Sanderson and Warner Fabrics to reissue patterns they had produced years before. Some wallpapers were designed to form a dado, a deep frieze, and a plainer middle section.

Parlour

The parlour has a dado of dark maroon – it could be embossed leather or a washable marbled paper. The woodwork and floorboards are stained dark brown. A gathered pelmet is fixed to the mantelpiece of

The parlour is crammed with furniture, including an upright piano, and has to double as the dining room

a tiled fireplace, with a painted wood or metal surround and a lower grate than the earlier designs. The enclosed grate regulates the draught and the fire can be kept burning slowly. The firebricks replacing the metal backplate throw more heat back into the room. The tiled hearth is surrounded by a cast-iron fender.

A clock under a dome and some Staffordshire figures stand on the mantelpiece. The mahogany sideboard, or chiffonier, against the back wall is cluttered with more ornaments. China, glass, table linen and cutlery are stored inside.

Near the window a round table covered in a dark cloth is used for reading and working. It is laid for tea with a white tablecloth and a pink

floral tea service that tones with the colours of the room. The silver tea set would probably be Sheffield plate in this household. The balloon back dining chairs are more delicate than those seen in the previous nursery, being a revival of an earlier style.

A buttonback sofa and chair pick up the peach colour in the wallpaper. There is even room for an upright piano in the corner. If it is not used much a collection of ornaments and photographs will accumulate on top, the woodwork protected by a lace-edged runner.

Pictures may be sentimental or of hunting scenes. Prints of Landseer's 'Monarch of the Glen' (a large stag) were very popular. Pretty girls of no background were

painted by Millais and other portrait painters, and when hundreds of prints were sold the girls became celebrities in society, like the fashion models and film stars of today.

An Indian carpet covers the centre of the floor. Various Indian ornaments have been brought back by relatives working in India, in the army or in commerce – a buddha, carved ivory or ebony elephants, and brass vases.

Potted plants may stand in the bay window, framed by lace curtains. A plain, red velvet curtain is drawn at night. The room is lit by a pair of gas wall lights. Movable oil lamps are used for reading.

Hall

The hall is too narrow for any furniture except a cast-iron umbrella stand and a hall mirror with coat hooks. The stair carpet could be Indian, but this might clash with the floor tiles and the floral carpet blends better with the wallpaper. There is a small light at the back of the hall, and on the first floor landing.

Bathroom

Upstairs a tiled bathroom contains a cast-iron bath and a china basin, boxed-in with wooden panelling. Hot and cold running water comes from a lead storage tank in the roof, and a hot water tank behind the kitchen range. The flush toilet is in the basement where it is easier to plumb. A frosted glass panel in the door lights the corridor. Net curtains or a blind over the window can be drawn for privacy. There is a wall light on the back wall.

Bedroom

The bedroom has the same dark woodwork as the parlour, and the floor is unstained. The walls have a patterned dado with a small all-over pattern for the centre, and a small border below the cornice.

An up-to-date cast-iron fireplace warms the room. There is no need for a washstand, but there is a bedside cupboard for the chamber pot. The cast-iron and brass bedstead has casters and can easily be moved for cleaning. A patchwork quilt matches the colours in the wallpaper.

A dressing table and mirror stand near the window, with a brush, comb and mirror set. A wardrobe,

The cast iron bath and porcelain basin are boxed in with wooden panelling

The narrow entrance hall is decorated with William Morris wallpaper

69

Cast iron beds without heavy drapery are now considered more hygienic, and carpets are no longer fitted

chest of drawers with a shaving mirror, and a small buttonback chair complete the furniture.

There is a gas light on the back wall. If any extra light is needed in the evening a pair of candlesticks or a portable oil lamp may be used on the dressing table or the mantelpiece.

Lace curtains veil the window, and a heavier curtain hangs on a brass or wooden cornice pole.

Attic

The attic can be used for the children or servants. A bedside rug is laid on the scrubbed wooden floor between the two pine beds, which might have patchwork, crochet or quilted covers, or a printed cotton throw.

A small pine washstand with a ewer and basin will be used for a cold wash, while a potty is hidden in the bedside cupboard. There is space for a small wardrobe and a chest of drawers, and a toy chest. The sloping walls and dormer window are covered in a small-patterned paper.

Basement

The basement is separated from the hall by a matchboarded partition and a glazed door – to keep in the smell of cooking. A solid stone staircase, with iron banisters and handrail, leads down to the entrance lobby. A stone sink is near the outside door, and in a small room under the stairs is a boxed-in toilet, with a flush plunge handle.

Kitchen

The protective matchboarding continues in the corridor and kitchen. For once, the scullery and kitchen can be separate. A plate rack would hang over the sink, which has a cold tap. Hot water would be drawn from the stove.

The oval wooden washtub is used for washing clothes, with a washing dolly or a posser to thump the dirt out. The servant can work in the kitchen near the hot water, or in the basement area in good weather. A wringer can be screwed to the side of the tub to squeeze out the water, with the sheets and clothes collecting in a clean bucket or basket underneath.

The matchboard, dresser and fire surround can be painted or stained light brown. A scrubbed-top table stands in the centre, and all food preparation, including rolling pastry or kneading bread, is carried out here. Dough could be left to rise on a table under the window.

The floor is of terracotta quarry tiles, so a rope mat or a wooden duckboard (a plank supported on two cross pieces) is warmer to stand on, and a rag rug might lie in front of the range by the maid's wicker armchair, which is lined with quilted patchwork.

The dresser has a good selection of decorative china, teapots and storage jars. The tea caddies are stored near the fireplace to keep them dry, and a pair of Staffordshire dogs stand on the mantelpiece. There may also be souvenir plates and postcards.

The Family

The family living in the house are unpretentious. The husband could be a bank clerk, or may work in an office like Mr Pooter in Diary of a Nobody who lived in a similar house in North London.

There is only one servant, a maid, who cleans and helps with the plainer cooking. She probably lives nearby, as the attic bedroom is used by the children.

Water for washing is heated on the kitchen range, the sink is in the lobby scullery

Making and Decorating the House

You will need:

- made-up or kit doll's house, kit basement, dormer window (mass-produced or kit)
- 2 glazed doors (for bathroom and stairs) and a four-panel door (for toilet)
- 'frosted glass' cut from polythene plastic milk bottles or plastic food cartons
- clear plastic glazing for the other windows
- ready-made basement stairs or $3/4$ in (19 mm) triangle and $1/8$ in (3 mm) panel to cut your own or $3/4 \times 1 1/2$ in (19 x 38 mm) wood, cut and stepped
- moulded quarry tiles for basement floor (optional)
- printed paper flagstone for area and pavement (optional)
- black and white and blue and white vinyl sheet floor tiles
- sheets of moulded brick (optional)
- roofing: cut strips of card or use MDF sheets
- white acrylic primer or emulsion
- emulsion paint sample pots: old white or lime white, mahogany, wainscot
- tube of black acrylic paint
- cream paint (Farrow & Ball satin)
- gloss enamel in the following colours: green (for front door), black (for basement stair banisters), & steel (for basement lights)
- sheets of wooden flooring (optional)
- $1/16$ in (1.5 mm) sheet or ply (for matchboarding)
- $1/16 \times 1/8$ in (1.5 x 3 mm) strip (for dado rail and basement handrail)
- $1/16$ in (1.5 mm) dowel or cocktail sticks (for basement banisters)
- skirting and cornice
- assorted wallpapers
- wood glue and wallpaper paste
- $3/4 \times 1 1/2$ in (19 x 38 mm) wood (to join house to base)
- Stanley or craft knife
- self-heal cutting mat
- metal straight edge or raised ruler
- wiring and lights – copper strip, wire, large or small eyelets
- 12 amp transformer

Cutting the Openings

The doll's house pictured was ready assembled. The basement was made up from a separate kit.

1. Remove the hinges from the roof and the front before decorating.
2. Cut a hole in the roof to fit the assembled dormer window. Do this by tracing around the dormer and cutting $3/8$ in (10 mm) inside the line.
3. If you prefer to have a lift-off roof (essential if you are adding decorative ridge tiles), add a horizontal $1/2$ in (13 mm) square strip to act as a catch against the front wall of the attic.
4. Cut square the curved opening on the first floor to fit a glazed bathroom door.
5. Cut chimney breasts if needed from solid wood, or make up from balsa and card or ply and wood. Remember to continue the chimney breast through the attic.

Basement

1. Paint and distress the basement ceiling and walls, or prime if wallpapering later. They would be stained with soot from the coal fire but could have been whitewashed recently.
2. Paint flagstones or black and white tiles on the floor, or add moulded quarry tiles after the staircase and dividing wall have been fitted.
3. Assemble the base, back and side walls of the box. The ceiling cannot be fixed until the stairwell is measured and cut out.
4. Try the made-up staircase in the main hall and mark with a pencil where it fits. The line up the wall will give the angle of the partition.
5. Cut the hole for the basement stairs about $1/4$ in (6 mm) narrower than the stairs to allow for the partition and skirting, and $1 1/2$ in (38 mm) from the back wall to form a landing when the top step is added. When you fit the basement stairs you will have to cut away some of the extra $1/4$ in (6 mm) to fit the top step. A ready-made staircase $2 1/2$ in (6.4 cm) wide x 9 in (30 cm) high fitted this house exactly. You can make your own from a $3/4$ in (19 mm) angle glued to a $1/8$ in (3 mm) backing strip or $2 1/2 \times 1 1/2 \times 3/4$ in (64 x 38 x 19 mm) stepped like stone blocks.
6. Cut a matching hole in the basement ceiling the full $2 1/2$ in (6.4 cm) wide plus a little extra to allow for the overlap into the wall, and 6 in (15 cm) long to allow for headroom.
7. Check the staircase will fit through the opening before fixing the ceiling. Stand the house on the basement and check the height of the stairs, widening the opening in the hall floor to fit the top step.
8. Cut card patterns to try out the angle under both staircases (which should be 45 degrees). Mark where the hall door and toilet door will fit. Cut a doorway in the interior kitchen wall.

Decoration

You can decorate most of the house and basement before joining them. The hall and palour floors can be laid afterwards to cover any screws or pins.

1. Electric wiring tape should be attached before decorating. If using wire, some removable sockets or eyelets may have to be fixed on side

**Curtains on a brass rod
cover the lace curtains**

walls before papering; ceiling lights can be run to the back wall before the cornice is glued; lights on the back wall simply need holes drilled through; on the outside wall the wire can be hidden in a groove under the brickwork or inside behind the paper. Run wires for table lamps behind skirtings and fireplaces.

2   Prime all surfaces to be painted or papered using acrylic primer or matt emulsion. Use old white or lime white on the ceilings. Be careful not to mark any floors that will not be covered. You can draw floorboards with a black biro or, for plain boards in the attic, a brown felt-tip pen. Stain and varnish the parlour floor, or add wood flooring to all rooms later.

3   Paint or stain lengths of skirting, cornice, dado rail and doors. Use white or off-white for the bathroom, medium brown for the basement, and chocolate brown upstairs. Paint

the stairs and banisters. The basement stairs are stone, so can be white or grey. Mix yellow ochre, black and white for an authentic colour. Their black metal banisters will be added later.

Hall

1   Make tongue-and-groove matchboarding for the hall. To allow for a $^1/_2$ in (13 mm) skirting, cut 2 $^1/_2$ in (6.4 cm) strips of $^1/_{16}$ in (1.5 mm) obeche, spruce or plywood across the grain. Score grooves $^1/_2$ in (13 mm) apart along the grain with a fine screwdriver or blunted bradawl. Cut the panels, skirting and $^1/_{16} \times ^1/_8$ in (1.5 x 3 mm) dado rail to fit the hall, ready to be glued once the basement stairs are fixed. Cut matchboard panels to fit under the stairs and up to the door post. Paint matt mahogany. A gloss or varnished finish will show up the grain and the grooves will be lost. Polish to give a sheen.

2   The coloured (encaustic) tiles are made by filling in some of the pattern of a black and white vinyl sheet with brown and ochre felt-tip pens or markers. The border can follow the outside walls only or run around the staircase as well. Lay the tiles after the house is joined to the basement.

Wallpapers

If possible, choose all your wallpapers at the same time so you can co-ordinate your colour scheme with the more limited colours available for upholstered furniture. Pale upholstery can be changed with a felt-tip pen or with paint.

Parlour

1   In the parlour draw a dado line 3 in (7.6 cm) high. Cut the paper about 2 $^3/_4$ in (7 cm) high to allow room to glue the skirting to bare wood.

2   Paste the marbled dado around the room. Include the chimney breast before the fireplace is fixed. You can cut and overlap at the corners as described in the previous chapter but you may be able to paste one continuous strip. Butt up the patterned paper above it and glue the dado rail over the join. Use a strip of 3 in (7.6 cm) card to keep it straight.

3   Drill holes for the wall lights and table lamp after checking where the furniture will fit.

Bedroom

Wallpaper the bedroom. A strip of border paper has been used for the dado and border, and a strong all-over pattern for the middle section. Cut sheets of floorboards to fit the bedroom and parlour. You should use scrubbed wood for the bedroom and a dark stained wood for the parlour. Some sheets have adhesive under the paper backing while others need gluing. Make sure the doors will open over the extra thickness. Fix the cast-iron fireplace after cutting black paper to fit within the fender.

Corridor

Paper the corridor upstairs. Drill and fit a light on the back wall, and drill the back wall for the wire from the bathroom light before fitting the bathroom and bedroom doors. Paper the hall down to the dado rail. The stairs will be glued firmly to the hall floor and top landing later, when the basement is attached. Drill for the hall light.

Bathroom

The vinyl flooring is the same pattern as the hall, printed in blue. Paper the walls with tile paper. You can use plain tiles for the top section. Fix the light to the back wall of the bathroom. Cut a panel of opaque plastic for the bathroom door from a plastic milk bottle or food container. (The top of the door pulls up to release the glazing.)

Attic

Paper the attic. The floor is left bare with the floorboards having been drawn with a felt-tip pen. Alternatively, use natural wood flooring. Skirting is unnecessary.

Basement

1   Make matchboarding to fit around the walls and up to the sink, and a panel under the stairs. Paint light brown (wainscot).
2   Check the position of the stairs and the width needed for the toilet door.

Allow for a $\frac{3}{8}$ in (10 mm) square post each side, one fixed to the kitchen wall and the other to the matchboarding. Pin and glue the internal wall top and bottom and at the back to line up with the parlour wall.

3   Fix the chimney breast before laying the vinyl quarry tiles. The lobby tiles will be fitted later, when the stairs are fixed.
4   Drill the back wall of the toilet for a light. Use a hidden bulb or a candlestick. Fix a gas light near the sink (paint the brass bracket with steel or silver Humbrol enamel). Run the wire along the ceiling to the back or drill a hole and take the wire out on top of the basement.
5   As there is not much headroom the kitchen will need one or two wall lights (also painted steel which is more suitable than brass for a kitchen) and possibly candles or an oil lamp.
6   Join the basement to the house. Glue and pin battens front and back to fill

the space between the floor and ceiling. Leave a gap for any wires from the basement lights. Two vertical battens across the join at the back will strengthen it.

Stairs

1   Cut $\frac{3}{8}$ in (10 mm) square door frames for both doors.
2   Fix the glazed hall door to open inwards over the stairs (Fig 55).
3   Add $\frac{1}{4}$ in (6 mm) batten to the underneath of both stairs, $\frac{1}{4}$ in (6 mm) from the edge.
4   Glue the hall skirting and matchboarding to a triangle of card or ply, with a batten along the bottom, and fit under the stairs to butt up to the batten and the basement door frame. Glue the stairs and panel in place.
5   Add matchboard panels to the hall walls. Cut away to fit over the bottom treads. Keep the dado rail level with a 3 in (7.6 cm) strip of card until dry.

Fig. 55 Glazed hall door

Fig. 56 Basement stairs

6   Cut a panel to make a toilet wall the width of the basement stairs, paper the toilet with plain tiles and cut the quarry tiles to fit around the bottom of the stairs, up to the wall and inside the toilet.

7   Fix the lighting inside, and run the wire from the still unattached light by the sink over the kitchen door and out of the back.

8   Make an 'iron' banister for the basement stairs with $^1/_{16}$ in (1.5 mm) dowel or cocktail sticks for uprights and a $^1/_{16}$ x $^1/_8$ in (1.5 x 3 mm) handrail, painted gloss black.

9   Glue the wall panel, stairs and matchboarding in position (Fig 56). You can cut a cupboard door in it if you wish, opening on black strap hinges.

10 As the toilet door has to open outwards, against the stairs, the door frame is built up once the door is in place, and the architrave is added on the outside.

Exterior

1   Paint the front steps and area steps matt white.

2   Paint all the mouldings, the edges of the windows and basement walls dark cream. (I have cut plain basement window sills $^1/_4$ in (6 mm)

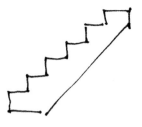

Fig. 57 Lead flashing

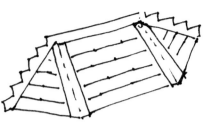

Fig. 58 Lead on bay

square and left off the lintels.)

3   Paint the windows chocolate-brown. Cut sheets of moulded vinyl bricks to fit, matching the brick courses at the joins. Use quick-drying wood glue. Cover the front, sides, and around the bays.

4   You can use sheets of MDF roofing for the tiles. Glue one sheet at a time to make sure the edges are stuck. You may need to pin it until dry. Leave space round the opening for the dormer to fit. Tile the dormer. Finish the ridge with wooden ridge tiles or a length of birdmouth angle partly cut through and paint the roof slate grey. If you make zig-zag ridge tiles (from card cut into points with a knife or pinking shears) paint them terracotta.

5   The bay has lead flashing. It is easier to cut this from ruled paper. Cut a strip about $^3/_4$ in (19 mm) wide to

match the angle, keeping the lines horizontal. Draw $^1/_4$ in (6 mm) steps along the top edge (Fig 57), paint light matt grey (the oxidised colour of weathered lead) and glue to fit over the bricks and under the tiles. Cut a straight strip for the top. When the three panels of tiles are joined, 'waterproof' the two joins with a $^3/_8$ in (10 mm) strip of paper (Fig 58).

6   Assemble the front section of the basement, making sure it lines up with the front of the house.

7   Now you can hang the front. Use a piano hinge or small flat hinges instead of cranked hinges. To stop the front catching on the base, rest it on a thin piece of card while fitting the hinge. If you wish to hinge the roof, cranked hinges can be used. Cut a $^3/_8$ in (10 mm) square prop to keep it open horizontally. If it flaps back the ridge will be damaged.

Slate roof with leading on the bay to waterproof the joints.

EDWARDIAN HOUSE, EARLY 1900S

CHAPTER SIX

Edwardian house, early 1900s

Interior of an Edwardian house, decorated with mass-produced furniture in convincing period style, with electric lighting

EDWARDIAN houses evolved in a variety of styles after returning to the mock 'vernacular' styles (in local materials) popularized by Charles Voysey and Edwin Lutyens. They were built of red brick or faced with stucco, sometimes textured with pebbledash and with mock-Tudor studwork. There were gables and bays, balconies and verandahs, and sometimes the bay projected below the gable. Front doors often had stained-glass panels, with more glass panels, or lights, on either side to light the hall.

Rows of detached or semi-detached houses sprang up in leafy suburbs or within commuting distance in the country, set in spacious gardens. Fewer servants were available, but with the labour-saving devices of electric lighting, and, in many places, gas fires, many households managed with just one or two daily servants.

The houses were solidly built, with damp courses and usually no basement. The roofs were mostly of slate, with red ridge tiles sometimes decorated with holes or a zig-zag, and gryphon finials.

Barge boards could be very fancy, sometimes cut into Gothic arches.

Inside, the houses were much lighter and brighter than before. Edward VII reigned from 1901 to 1910, but the Edwardian style covers a longer period. The release from heavy Victorian clutter was influenced by William Morris and his Arts and Crafts Movement which began in the 1860s, and eventually filtered to the general public through the work of the Silver Studio who designed wallpapers and fabrics for mass-production.

The emphasis was on hygiene, with large windows and plenty of light and although some were of stained glass, the heavy drapes were gone. Curtains were plain pulls, sometimes just muslin with a roller blind.

The woodwork was white, as were some suites of bedroom furniture and the new fitted cupboards. Walls lost their dados, except sometimes in the hall to protect the wall from passing traffic. Decorative deep friezes were now more popular.

In a detached house, there was room for the hall to open out and become an informal space one could linger in, instead of passing through as a corridor. There could be recesses, a raised platform by the window, and a cubby hole round the fire. The staircase became more prominent and a feature of the room, instead of being tucked away at the back. Staircases were usually built of unstained light oak. The hall was often used for dining, reverting to the traditional open hall of the medieval timber-framed houses, complete with panelling and heraldic designs.

Parquet floors were popular, covered with a few oriental rugs and wild animal skins brought back by big game hunters from Africa and India. Stuffed animal heads or antlers hung on the walls. My grandfather's house had a large gloomy hall with about twenty heads and antlers, trophies of stags shot in Scotland in the early 1900s.

Although the ground floor of his house had electric lighting, even by the 1940s he had not bothered to have the rest of the house wired and we had to carry lighted candles up to bed. In contrast my maternal grandfather wired up his father's house in 1888, at the age of eight! It was probably not as dangerous

as it sounds, as a lighting circuit was only 3 amps, using little 2-pin plugs. Stronger currents, for electric fires and cookers, were to come later, in the 1920s.

Cast-iron stoves were still used, burning coal or anthracite. A 'portable' range on legs did not need a fire surround, just a pipe extracting the smoke. Food and china were stored in glazed cupboards instead of on open shelves and dressers. The kitchen walls were usually tiled, at least to head height, and the floor covered in quarry tiles or linoleum.

The bathroom too was tiled on the floors and walls. Instead of being boxed in, pipes were

accessible and chromed to keep them bright. The taps were usually chromed, as brass needs daily polishing. The high cistern was made of wood with a lead lining, or of cast iron. Before pre-formed galvanized water tanks were made, storage tanks were made up from sheets of lead brazed together and fitted in odd spaces under the stairs or in the loft.

The bedrooms had polished floors and bedside rugs. Beds were wooden, or cast iron painted black or white, for children or servants. There was a vogue for matching sets of bedroom furniture, and fitted cupboards and wardrobes. Dressing table sets of silver-topped

The cook has been churning butter in the kitchen

The attic is used for the nurseries and storage. The nanny and children have to keep outdoor clothes upstairs. On the first floor, the young girl's bed roller blinds in place of curtains.

Nursery

matching white furniture. The bathroom fixtures are made up from a plastic kit, plus a metal 'bentwood' chair. The master bedroom has plain

glass jars for hairpins, creams, jewellery, and matching brush, comb and mirror, were essential.

A hot-water boiler (usually in an outside shed to keep the fumes out of the house) could be used for central heating through large cast-iron radiators and even for a heated towel rail in the bathroom.

Fireplaces were ornate and either of wood or cast iron, with a low grate lined with firebricks which throw the heat back into the room more efficiently than cast-iron firebacks. Ventilation underneath was controlled by an adjustable front to the ash pan.

The new electric lighting seemed harsh, and was hidden behind fringed shades of pleated silk, or beads.

Furniture was of mahogany or oak, and often reproductions of antique styles. The drawing-room furniture was fairly delicate, often inlaid, and no longer covered in cloths and ornaments (which were displayed in glazed cabinets and on the overmantel).

A horn gramophone supplied more choice of music than a piano (although some pianos were fitted with paper rolls of music which could be played automatically if the piano were not being played normally). Musical evenings were still popular. Barber shop quartets were an American craze, and music hall songs were often sung. Lawn tennis was played in long skirts, and most houses had a box of croquet mallets and balls near the back door, among the coats and boots.

Mass-produced metal toys were widely available – brass and tin-plate trains and cars, and lead soldiers. The upright teddy bear was invented in 1903; before this bears were more realistic and stood on all fours. Porcelain-headed dolls were replacing the wax and wooden ones. Wooden toys were still available, in all price ranges, from painted rocking horses to carved penny toys.

Dresses were slim and elegant, and drawn back to a slight bustle. Sleeves were tight, starting off puffed at the top and widening towards the cuff. Hair was piled up and padded. Girls wore black stockings and pinafores with their hair tied back in a bow. Boys had short trousers and matching jackets and caps, like the children in the E. Nesbitt stories often seen on television.

Dining hall with a brass gong on a side table, and animal skins on the floor . The drawing room has delicate furniture and glazed display cabinets.

MAKING AND DECORATING THE HOUSE

The house pictured is a typically American design with a raised verandah so familiar from films where the granny sat in her rocking chair, and where the young couple whispered good-night.

Transformed from a wooden building to brick, with a black and white tiled verandah, it now looks very English. To keep the American look you can cover it in clapboard (weatherboard). Hardwood strips are available, or a $^1/_2$ in (19 mm) trailing edge balsa, which tapers from $^1/_{16}$ to $^1/_8$ in (1.5 – 3 mm), can be butted up instead of overlapping. You can use 6 x 31 in (15 x 78 cm) sheets of MDF,

like the roofing sheets, but it may be hard to cut out so many windows.

This model comes in ready-assembled panels that only take half an hour to peg and screw together. (A more detailed American kit comes in plain panels with optional details of windows, trim, and cladding.) Similar houses with bays and dormers can be decorated in the same way.

You will need:

- made-up or kit doll's house
- acrylic primer or white emulsion, white and grey vinyl silk, olive and cream emulsion
- red brick paper
- spirit wood stain and white spirit
- sheets of moulded brick (optional)
- wallpapers and paste
- parquet and black and white floor paper
- brown (raw sienna) felt-tip pen
- $^1/_4$ in (6 mm) panels (for new walls)
- 4-panel bedroom door
- plain staircase or blocks for making one
- $^1/_8$ in (3 mm) dowel, $^1/_{16}$ in (1.5 mm) square strip, and muslin (for blinds)
- material and rods (for curtains)
- skirting and cornice
- wood glue

General tips

Assemble the house first, then label the panels by writing on a strip of masking tape before dismantling them for decorating so you will know which side of a wall is bathroom, bedroom, etc. Originally there were two rooms on each floor, plus a bathroom, and no access to the attic. I have added another partition, with a large opening on the ground floor to make a dining hall and sitting room and made a second bedroom with a steep staircase behind it to the attic.

This style of house could have French windows at the back, giving views of

extensive gardens (as in E. M. Forster's Howard's End), and a front door decorated with stained glass. These would have to be built from scratch, as ready-made doors will not fit.

The bay has been continued to the ground; originally the base was level with the verandah, and supported on brackets. The rather chunky construction of this house does not lend itself to fine detail and expensive brick treatment, so I have mostly used mass-produced furniture and papers, which suit it admirably.

Traditional red brick paper, the flat red with a ruled white line, has been used on doll's houses since the 1880s. The current garish red can be toned down with a thin solution of spirit wood stain, diluted with white spirit. Applied to the papered walls with a soft brush or cotton wool it gives a very mellow effect.

Before brick papering, the panels must be primed with acrylic primer or emulsion and the woodwork must be painted white. Gloss paints were used at this period, so a satin or silk finish is best. The pillars and railings on the porch take some time. You may need a short paint brush to reach behind them.

You need to work out structurally which parts would be brick and which white. The dormer over the bay would be brick, but the smaller one is only supported by the roof and not an outside wall, so would be plaster over a wooden framework or weatherboard. The triangular support at the sides of the verandah roof, and the wall of the balcony, could only be wood as they are supported on slender wooden pillars.

The external doors can be left plain. They would have been varnished or wood-grained, or they could be darkened to contrast with the brick.

Preparation

The new partitions can be cut to fit once the house is assembled, but you must cut the access hole in the attic floor 2 x 4 $^1/_2$

in (5 x 11 cm) and $^3/_4$ in (19 mm) in from the frame. This will allow for a very steep staircase, running across the back window. Cut $^1/_4$ in (6mm) panels to fill in the base of the bay, strengthening with battens or blocks.

Prime all surfaces except the top two floors (the ground floor will be papered), the staircase, the two support posts at the front of the floors, the matching posts hinged to the front, and the front base. The attic's interior roof can be painted, papered later, or left as plain wood.

Paint the windows, internal doors, the sides of the base and all exterior woodwork white. Also paint the cornice and skirting strips on the panels. Keep the labels on the dry surfaces as a reminder of how the panels fit together.

Check where the walls will fit, and paint the bathroom floor. Use a shiny parquet paper for the hall and drawing-room floor, and black and brown 'quarry tiles' for the kitchen (use a black and white paper coloured with a raw sienna felt-tip pen). The tiles could also be yellow and brown, or all brown.

Wallpaper

Plan your colour scheme and lay the wallpapers next to each other to check that they complement each other rather than clash. The patterns here are rather strong and linear; typical of the period. The $^1/_2$ in (13 mm) kitchen wall tiles were drawn on buff paper.

Paper the walls before assembling, so you can cut accurately round the windows. Leave spare paper at the corners which can be cut back to a slight overlap later. Paper the tiled bathroom floor and walls.

Assemble the house. You will need to peg the back into the base, then slide most of the panels together at once – first floor, outside walls and bathroom.

Partitions and stairs

Cut the new partitions. The bedroom wall runs to the end of the stairwell, replacing the left-hand banister. Cut a doorway $^1/_2$ in (13 mm) from the front post. Cut the back bedroom wall, remembering to cut it shorter where it fits under the ceiling framework.

Make a steep staircase 2 $^1/_2$ in (6.4 mm) or 2 $^1/_4$ in (5.7 mm) wide from $^3/_4$ in (19 mm) triangle on $^1/_{16}$ in (1.5 mm) or $^1/_8$ in (3 mm) strip. To use at a steeper slope than

45 degrees the steps can be kept horizontal with a $^1/_8$ in (3 mm) spacer (Fig. 59). Cut the bottom steps away to fit the wall framework. Glue white painted $^1/_4$ in (6 mm) square 'skirtings' to the inside of the walls to match the construction elsewhere and to act as battens when fixing.

Fit the walls along the stairwell and the stairs. When the back wall of the bedroom is fixed against the stairs it will need to be kept firm against a block of wood in the bottom left-hand corner, cut to the same depth as the stairs. Cut the front banister to fit.

Wallpaper the new walls. The overlap in the corners will strengthen the joints. Cut away the paper from the doorway and fix the door. Add the stair carpet, and lay some to the bedrooms.

Cut the opening in the hall partition. This one is 8 in high x 6 $^1/_2$ in (20 x 16 cm) wide, but you can vary the size. Glue a white painted $^1/_4$ in (6 mm) strip along the top edge, and another to the ceiling, and glue the partition between them, centred on the two square uprights front and back.

Complete the house

Cut away the wallpaper to fit all the corners with a slight overlap. Add skirting to match the $^1/_4$ in (6 mm) strips. On the ground floor ordinary skirting can be used. In the drawing room it is olive green instead of the usual white, to give a strong edge to the wall against the parquet. Paper the inside of the fronts to line up with the interior.

Make roller blinds from a short length of upholstery tape (to give you selvedges) glued to $^1/_8$ in (3 mm) dowel and $^1/_{16}$ in (1.5 mm) square batten (Fig 60), and green silk curtains for the drawing room and dividing wall. Glaze the windows to keep out dust.

Brick the exterior with paper distressed with wood stain, or use thin sheets of moulded brick. Paint the roof dark grey, and add chimneys, to be removed when the attic is opened.

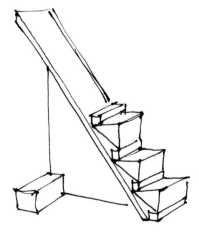

Fig. 59 Attic stairs

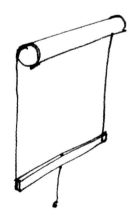

Fig. 60 Roller blind

Bay window of drawing room with gramophone and a leopard skin rug.

Furnishing details

The decorative fireplace has adhesive tiles added to the hearth and side panels. You can make a leopard skin rug from printed fabric cut to shape and pasted on to a slightly larger piece of black cotton (Fig 61). More detailed animal skins are made by stitching loops through fabric with a punch needle, gluing the back and trimming the loops level.

A painted gramophone pencil sharpener can look most realistic, and brass jardinieres and plant stands are less garish if painted gold or brass. The interiors of the kitchen cupboard and the display cabinet have been painted (cream and green) to display the contents.

A hanging light shade can be made with a brass bracket, a 1 in (2.5 cm) ring and green silk. Suspend on three cords pulled level through a small ring, hang a bulb in the centre and fix to the ceiling (Fig 62). If wiring this house, flat copper tape can be run to the back of each panel and joined after assembly.

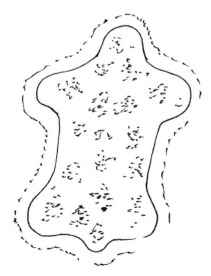

Fig. 61 Leopard skin rug

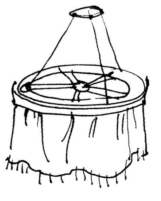

Fig. 62 Hanging light

CHAPTER SEVEN

Suburban House, 1930s

Interior of a typical 1930s suburban house, decorated in shades of cream and green. Most of this furniture is handmade.

IN the 1930s there was a great exodus to the suburbs. With the growth of the London Underground, 'Metroland', as described by John Betjeman, engulfed acres of farmland occupied by people who could not afford to live in town and had to move beyond the spacious Edwardian properties to Acton and Park Royal, Romford and Perivale.

Most big towns were surrounded by suburban developments of two-storey brick houses, often finished in a nostalgic style of 'Olde England', now known as by-pass Tudor, which usually meant adding a few black studs and beams over the pebbledash on the first floor. Typical characteristics of these houses were a hipped roof, pebbledash finish, a

gabled bay, tile hanging, and a porch. Some roofs were of green pantiles, and some shiny red tiles eventually weathered almost black.

Doll's houses of the period illustrate the current style – Triang, with their double-gabled fronts, and Hobbies plans with intricate fretwork studwork to be used over sandpaper pebbledash. It is only recently that doll's houses have not reflected the architecture of the time – in the 1960s and 1970s Lundby and Barton were making Scandinavian style houses with one roof slope longer than the other. Now there is nostalgia for the past, in furnishing as well as architecture, and very little modern architecture to copy. Even toy plastic houses are being made by Playmobil in the style of a French chateau.

There are some 1930s style doll's houses available, but the the house illustrated has been adapted from my book Build a Doll's House, using the same kit as the stone house in Chapter Two. The sides of the roof were cut back to make a hipped roof. A bay window was added under an extended dormer; the original window holes being extended and filled in where necessary.

To make space for a bathroom, one bedroom wall was moved across to leave a corridor, and the bathroom fitted in front of the stairs between the two bedrooms (Fig 63). The basic size of the house is 26 in (66 cm) wide × 12 in (30.5 cm) deep. You will need at least this depth to accommodate the bathroom and the staircase.

Paintwork

Inside dull shades of brown, green and cream were popular colours. Oil-based paint tended to turn yellow within a year – so people speeded the process by painting 'broken white' to start with! Kitchens were usually yellow and green. For a matching colour scheme through the house, hound lemon has been used in the kitchen and on all the ceilings, and lime white for the upstairs woodwork, instead of the warmer magnolia shades that would have clashed with the kitchen. The rest of the woodwork is painted brown or wood-grained.

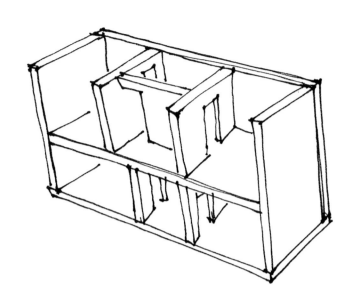

Fig. 63 Repositioning of bedroom wall

Floors

The hall and kitchen floors have 'linoleum' – made from parquet patterned paper. The living room (sitting-cum-dining) has real parquet panels. These come in packs of six, 2 × 6 in (5 × 15 cm), in contrasting tones. Use woodstain to even up the colour, so there is a texture but no two-tone effect. Make sure you stain the same side of each panel so that the pattern matches.

There is stained wood flooring in the bedroom and on the upstairs landing – this covers the joins where the floor is extended.

Bathroom

The bathroom has blue and white tiled 'lino' and painted and tiled walls (drawn on blue speckled paper). The cast-iron bath and high cistern could be used from late Victorian times up to the present day, as there is a vogue in reproduction cast-iron baths and high cisterns, which take up less room than a low flush. There is a wooden soap rack across the bath, and a chrome towel rail and toilet roll holder.

The free standing bath and high level toilet cistern would be cast iron

Living room

A yellow and green fern patterned paper gives a period feel to the living room. You might try copying some of the mottled beige papers with typically suburban angular patterns mixed with flowers – shades of Cubism softened with chintz!

A square tiled fireplace and hearth can be mottled in green or brown. Paint a cheap plastic mirror, or cut three tapered panels from mirror card. There are brass bellows and a companion set of tongs, shovel and poker. There could be a small brush as well, and a rag rug in front of the fire. A small electric fire, painted green, stands in the hearth. A folding cake stand is ready for tea, which the maid is bringing on the trolley.

A three-piece suite is covered in brown leather and has squashy tweed cushions. (These are filled with sand or rice, so sit heavily and can be dented realistically, unlike springy foam.) A brass ashtray sits on one arm, on a fringed leather strap. A clock sits on the sideboard, next to some books and a circular Bakelite radio.

As the room is small, the table is drop-leaf (though where it would open out I am not sure!). It has a set of hexagonal wooden mats. The furniture is oak, the dining chairs mock Cromwellian.

A galleon in full sail stands in the bay window, which has green curtains and a frilled pelmet.

Hall

The hall has brown anaglypta paper (tile pattern stained brown) along the dado and up the stairs. The rest is papered in a mottled cream. There is a row of coat hooks and a grandfather clock. The doors and stairs are woodgrained. The plain

The bedroom has a Lloyd Loom wicker cradle and armchair

The living room has comfortable leather furniture grouped around a green tiled fireplace stair carpet would be held with stair clips rather than rods.

Kitchen

The kitchen has a stone sink, with a geyser for hot water, and a gas cooker. A kitchen cabinet with let-down front and cupboards contains dry food. A meat safe with perforated zinc panels is used to keep flies off the meat and fish. Cotton or wire mesh covers were also used, and butter muslin covers weighted with beads protected the milk jugs. Pans and bowls are stored in another cupboard. An enamelled tin bread bin stands on top, and a bread slicer was very useful before the advent of sliced bread. The teapot would have a knitted or crocheted cosy.

Storage shelves and some work tops can be covered in American oil cloth – in a check pattern that can be wiped clean (varnish some curtain material). Green checked curtains hang on a rod over the windows, matching those under the sink.

A clothes airer hangs from the ceiling on a pulley. Striped pyjamas are drying on a folding clothes horse in front of an oil heater. The washing would be done by hand in the sink, using square bars of soap or the new washing powders Rinso and Lux. Some up-to-date houses might have a very basic washing machine, where the clothes were stirred with wooden paddles.

Electric kettles could be copper, or enamelled brown, cream or green, like the pans. The electric iron might

be plugged into the light fitting with a circular adapter, and a collapsible ironing board was easier to use than a table top. A toaster with let-down sides and a blackbird pie funnel are just like those my granny used to have.

Bedroom

The bedroom has rather dowdy yellow floral patterned paper. The curved bedroom suite with matching wardrobe, chest of drawers, bedside table and bedhead are very typical. A shiny counterpane covers the bed, a matching eiderdown could be on top or underneath. Hot-water bottles might be rubber or stoneware, with a knitted cover.

A fold-out workbox stands on the chest of drawers. There is a

The kitchen has a gas cooker and hot water geyser, a smocked dress is hanging from the clothes pulley. The tea trolley is very handy.

Lloyd Loom wicker chair and a baby's cot which could equally well have been used in the Edwardian house, but would not have fitted in the chunkier style of house.

The kidney dressing table by the window has a frill of fine cotton glued round the top edge. A piece of card, cut slightly larger than the top to hide the top of the frill, is covered in plain material. A 'glass' top is cut from clear plastic. A triple mirror has been made by adding mirror card to an angled brass fireguard (after snipping off the handles with pliers), and adding veneer or thin, stained wood to the back.

Plain tan curtains hang at the bay window with a frilled pelmet. Net curtains could be hung in each window. You can hang this fabric on shirring elastic tied to two pins – to simulate the coiled wire used for real net curtains.

The nursery is heated by a small electric fire

Nursery

The children's room has a 'cork' floor – use unstained MDF, an old cork mat, or a sheet of model railway cork. There is a striped wallpaper with a nursery rhyme frieze. The cast-iron beds have crochet covers. There is a cupboard and a chest of drawers. The boy would have toy trains, a wooden bi-plane or a balsa glider, lead soldiers and a fort, and a rocking horse. The girl's toys would be a doll's house, pram, china dolls, teddy, golly, felt rabbit. There is a goldfish bowl, a jar of tiddlers, a bucket and spade, and a shrimping net.

Lighting

An alabaster bowl on three chains hangs in the sitting room. Wall brackets with straight semi-circular shades could be used on the back wall or on either side of the fireplace. A wooden standard lamp with a gathered or slightly cone-shaped parchment shade can be moved where needed for reading or knitting. A frosted glass shade is fixed to the ceiling in the hall. There are small glass shades in the bathroom and in the corridor, and a pink one in the nursery. The kitchen has a white coolie shade, and in the bedroom there is a plain bedside light.

Standard lamp

MAKING AND DECORATING THE HOUSE

You will need:

- 4-room kit 26 in (66 cm) wide x 12 in (30 cm) deep (Basic House kit) or 4 x 8 ft (1.22 x 2.44 m) of $^3/_8$ in (10 mm) ply or MDF
- special windows and glazing
- 4 high panelled doors (or reverse mass-produced ones), glazed front door, glazed bathroom door
- plain bevelled skirting
- handrail and $^1/_4$ in (6 mm) square and $^1/_8$ in (3 mm) square (for newels and banisters)
- simple stair kit or $^3/_4$ in (19 mm) triangle strip & $^1/_{16}$ in (1.5 mm) panel (optional)
- $^1/_4$ in (6 mm) ply or MDF (for roof)
- balsa (for chimney and bay)
- parquet (for living room)
- parquet paper (for kitchen and hall)
- roofing sheets, chimney pots
- coarse sandpaper (for pebbledash)
- brick sheet
- grouting or Polyfilla
- wood flooring (for bedroom and upstairs landing)
- assorted wallpapers
- emulsion paint sample pots: hound lemon, lime white, pea green, wainscot (Farrow & Ball)
- terracotta acrylic paint (for roof)
- fabric glue
- brushes and paint roller

Preparation

Cut panels to the following sizes:
- back wall 17 $^5/_8$ x 26 in (44.8 x 66.6 cm)/front wall 16 $^1/_2$ x 26 in (41.9 x 66.6 cm)
- 2 x sides 12 x 17 $^5/_8$ in (30.5 x 44.6 cm)
- base 12 $^3/_8$ x 26 in (31.4 x 66.6 cm)
- top and floor each 12 x 25 $^1/_4$ in (30.5 x 64.1 cm)
- 2 x internal walls 12 x 6 $^1/_2$ in (30.5 x 16.5 cm)/1 x internal wall 12 x 17 $^1/_4$ in (30.5 x 43.8 cm)
- base strip 3 x 26 in (7.6 x 66.6 cm)/front strip 1 x 26 in (2.5 x 66.6 cm)
- 2 x roof panels $^1/_4$ in (6 mm) thick, 10 $^1/_4$ in x 27 $^1/_2$ in (26 x 69.8 cm)
- 2 x end panels 10 $^1/_4$ x 15 in (26 x 38 cm) angled to fit later

If adapting from a kit or plans:

1. First cut the sides square. Cut the gable triangles off level with the back panel. (They will be used later as roof trusses.)
2. Cut the base to the same depth as the walls plus the back. Cut a 3 in (7.6 cm) deep strip to fit under the front to support the bay.
3. Cut the left internal wall to ground floor ceiling height. The top wall will be moved to the left, with the doorway near the back wall.

Cutting the openings

1. Check all doors will fit their doorways.
2. When the stairs are made cut a stairwell, or strips to fill in, and the right-hand bedroom doorway. A $^3/_8$ in (3mm) slot from the front of the wall continues below the doorway to fit the front landing (Fig 64)
3. The windows will be cut once the house is assembled.

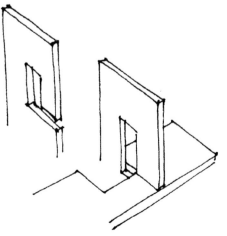

Fig. 64 Cut slot in wall to fit over landing

Decoration

1. Seal all internal walls and ceilings with acrylic primer or emulsion. Also seal any floors to be papered – the kitchen, hall and bathroom.
2. Paint the kitchen lemon yellow and pea green. Use masking tape and roll one colour. Wait until completely dry (at least half a day) before masking the painted surface to butt up the second colour. Paint a 1 $^1/_2$ in (3.8 mm) border in the living room (masking tape is not necessary), and all the ceilings lemon yellow.
3. Stain the bedroom floor and the landing corridor, or add stained wood flooring later which will hide the joins. Leave the nursery floor plain, to look like cork, or add a thin sheet of cork later (available from model railway shops).
4. Doors should have the smaller panels at the top. The architrave and skirting should be plain, just slightly bevelled. The woodwork downstairs can be dark varnished, or woodgrained. Paint it lime white upstairs. Fit a frosted glass panel (using a plastic milk bottle as on page 74) in the bathroom door and re-hang all except the kitchen door on the left (see page 48).

Staircase

1. Partially assemble the house so you can work out the staircase. Pin and glue the back to the base, with the walls taped in place to keep the join secure. Secure the left-hand wall.
2. Mark the position of the bottom flight against the right-hand internal wall. $^3/_4$ x 2 $^1/_4$ in (19 x 57 mm) wide steps from a ready-made kit were used. Try the door in place, and start the stairs beyond the architrave. You can make a 45 degree angle guide by folding a square of paper in half diagonally. Allow for a 2 in (5 cm) half landing including the top step.

Fig. 65 Staircase

The higher this flight goes the shorter the top flight across the back wall.

3 Before cutting the stairs to length, assemble the floor, kitchen and right-hand internal walls with tape. If the panels are already grooved they may stay in position with only the right-hand outside wall taped.

4 Check how your bathroom furniture will fit on the front landing. The bedroom wall must not move too close to the window. If necessary, the toilet might fit under the staircase. At 7 in (17.8 cm) wide x 4 $\frac{1}{4}$ in (10.8 cm) deep, this room is rather cramped.

5 Check how many steps are needed to reach the first floor from the half landing, and extend the landing corridor by about 1 in (2.5 cm) to fit and to allow room for the banister (Fig 65). These steps must be cut down to 2 in (5 cm) wide to fit the half landing.

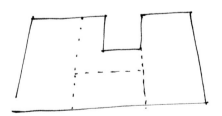

Fig. 66 Stairwell

6 The front landing must also be extended to form a corridor behind the bathroom. An extra 2 $\frac{1}{4}$ in (5.6 cm) will allow room for a door and the banisters. The front architrave will have to be removed and the bathroom wall butted up to the edge of the door. For cutting from scratch, cut the stairwell 4 in deep x 4 $\frac{5}{8}$ in wide (10 x 11.6 cm) to allow the right-hand wall to slot in to the floor, and the kitchen and nursery walls to fit between floors and ceilings (Fig 66).

7 Cut the new bedroom doorway. You can use the scrap wood plus Polyfilla to fill the original opening. Cut the bathroom wall 7 in (17.8 cm) wide with the doorway in the left corner. The glazed door will open to the left into the corridor.

8 Make good the ceiling in the hall, and fix top, right side and internal walls. (The bathroom wall will be fitted later.) Cover the landing with stained wood flooring.

9 Assemble the banisters. Use $\frac{1}{8}$ in (3 mm) square for the spindles and $\frac{1}{4}$ in (6 mm) square for the newels. Cut the top of the spindles at 45 degrees to make a better join to the handrail. The bottom flight can be fitted to the stairs. The landing banisters can be made in two strips with a bottom rail. Those on the second flight will need to be fitted in situ.

Wallpaper

1 Prepare the dado for the hall. A tile pattern darkened with woodstain was used to resemble anaglypta. Cut 3 in (7.6 cm) high for the hall and half landing and 2 in (5 cm) high for the angled side of the stairs.

2 Glue the small half landing in place, supported on scrap wood.

3 Draw the dado line in the hall and above the stairs, and paper down to it. Then add the hall dado, trimming about $\frac{1}{8}$ in (3 mm) off the bottom

before gluing the skirting in place.

4 Glue the stairs to the floor, wall and landing. Paint the wall above the treads to match the skirting, and paste the dado straight along the edge of the steps.

5 Add stair carpet with fabric glue, then assemble the banisters on the second flight to fit between the newels. Fix the banisters round the stairwell. Add carpet if necessary on the landing.

6 Parquet the living-room floor. 2 x 6 in (5 x 15 cm) wooden parquet blocks were used here, stained to an even colour. Make sure the door will open.

7 Use paper 'parquet' to look like linoleum in the hall and kitchen.

8 Paper the living room, fix the door, and add dark skirting and the picture rail. Glue the fireplace and hearth.

9 Add dark wood flooring to the bedroom. Wallpaper, and fix the door and skirting.

10 Wallpaper and finish the nursery.

11 Fix the bathroom wall. Paper the floor with blue and white tiles. Draw tiles on blue and white speckled paper for the wall tiles. Fix the door. (If lighting, run wires from the ceiling lights through the back.)

Hipped Roof

The roof panels join at a right angle. To work out the side panels of the hipped roof cut two cardboard panels to the size of the roof, 10 $\frac{3}{8}$ x 27 $\frac{1}{2}$ in (26.4 x 69.8 cm). Along the ridge mark the roof overhang $\frac{3}{4}$ in (19 mm) from each end. From there measure the same distance as the height of the gable triangle – this is 6 in (15 cm) (Fig 67). Cut the roof from this apex to the bottom corner. You can double-check the measurement when you mock up the roof by hinging at the ridge with tape and supporting on the gable triangles, taped to the top of the house (Fig 68).

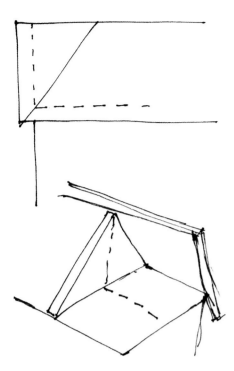

Fig. 67 Angle of hipped roof

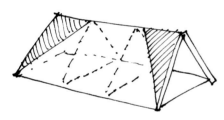

Fig. 68 Support roof

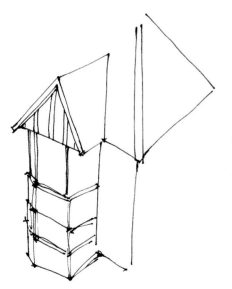

Fig. 69 Bay

Cut two card triangles with an approx 15 in (38 cm) base, 13 in (33 cm) sides, and 10 $\frac{1}{4}$ in (26 cm) height to fit each end. When you have checked that the card panels fit, cut them in 1/4 in (6 mm) ply or MDF and assemble with masking tape.

Mark the hole for the chimney in the right triangle flush with the outside wall. You can use a block of balsa $3 \times 1 \times 7$ in high ($7.6 \times 2.5 \times 17.8$ cm), so the chimney pots are above the ridge. Cut the hole and assemble the roof permanently, gluing and taping the panels with strips of fabric, resting on the gable triangles. Add the chimney later.

The gable over the bay will be planned with the bay window (Fig 69), and then the whole roof can be tiled.

Front

1 Arrange the windows on the front before cutting the openings. These were ready-made and typically 1930s, with small top windows 5 in (12.7 cm) high by 4, 2 $\frac{1}{2}$ & 5 $\frac{1}{2}$ in (10, 6.4, 14 cm) wide, and bays 6 in (15 cm) wide, 2 in (5 cm) deep, and 3 in (7.6 cm) in from the side. The first floor windows should be as near to the eaves as possible. The ground floor windows can be the same height as the door, or if slightly higher, allow for one course of bricks above it. Sheets of $\frac{1}{2}$ in (13 mm) and 1 in (25 mm) balsa are used to build up the bay. (If working on a kit, cut or fill in where necessary.)

2 Pin and glue the $\frac{3}{8} \times 3$ in (10×76 mm) deep base strip under the front.

3 Build up the bays, following the angles of the windows. When the brick cladding is added, they should be slightly wider than the windows and less than the sills. The bottom bay is 2 $\frac{1}{2}$ in (6.4 cm) high, the top 3 in (7.6 cm). Stack the parts in place to check the position of the dormer.

Plan the dormer

This can be flush with the front of the bay, but in this case has been set forward about 3/4 in (19 mm) to give the bay more prominence.

1 Cut a triangle of card just wider than the bay, with a right-angled apex about 4 in (10 cm) high by 8 in (20 cm) wide.

2 To work out the roof panels for the gable, hold the triangle vertically against the front edge of the roof and take a line at right angles from the apex to the roof. Draw a pencil line to each corner to find the angle of the roof triangles (Fig 70). These panels then extend 2 in (5 cm) to overhang the bays.

3 Cut two card roof panels, the right angles meeting at the apex of the triangle (Fig 71). Tape together and position over the bay, making sure that the dormer is not too close to the ridge of the side roof and is centred over the bay. Then fix the bay window; it is easier to re-align a dormer than a bay.

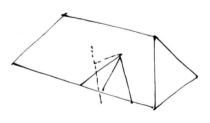

Fig. 70 Plan dormer roof

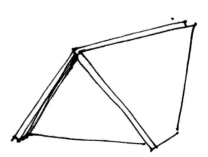

Fig. 71 Dormer roof panels

Bay windows and dormer roof

Front

Finish the front with plastic brickwork on the ground floor, and coarse sandpaper 'pebbledash' on the first floor. The bricks are moulded plastic sheets and need grouting. They have a shiny finish, very similar to the glazed bricks used so often in the 1930s, and like the toy Bako house-building kits.

Glue the bottom bay in position but fix the windows later over the brickwork. Brick up to the window and door surrounds, and up to the bay window opening. Remember to add a strip of bricks to the outside edges first and bring out the brick wall to cover them (Fig 72). Take the bricks up to the level of the top of the door and windows. Colour some grouting with black and yellow ochre, so it is not stark white (you can use Polyfilla). When the grouting is dry, wipe the excess off the bricks. You can restore some of the gloss to the bricks with cooking oil or shoe polish.

Glue the downstairs bay window and support the first floor bay on it. Glue sandpaper up to the window opening before gluing the bay windows and the panel above it. Cut the sandpaper from the back, the paper side, with a sharp knife. Join the sheets where least noticeable, at a window. You can disguise the join with weathering.

Add brick quoins. These are two bricks high alternating from one to one and a half brick's width (Fig 73).

Build the dormer

Cut the dormer panels from $^1/_4$ in (6 mm) ply or MDF. Glue a 1 in (2.5 cm) thick x 1 $^1/_2$ in (3.8 cm) deep piece of balsa (depending on your overhang) behind the base of the triangle, trimming the ends to an angle to fit (Fig 74). Glue a $^1/_4$ in (6 mm) square strip along the inside of one ridge to strengthen the join (Fig 75). Tape together and try on the roof, centred over the bay window. The roof panels project $^1/_4$ in (6 mm) over the triangle.

Glue the panels together firmly, using another $^1/_4$ in (6 mm) square strip to form the ridge, and glue on to the roof, strengthening the join with strips of fabric (Fig 76).

Roof

When the dormer is fixed, paint the joins grey (for lead gullies). Cut sheets of MDF roofing to fit. Wait for each panel to dry before gluing the next. Cover the ridges with a strip of wooden ridge tiles (birdmouth angle partially cut). Leave the opening for the chimney.

Paint the eaves and under the dormer green to match the windows. Paint the roof terracotta. Cover the dormer gable with sandpaper. Add $^1/_2$ x $^1/_{16}$ in (6 x 1.5 mm) strips of green studwork.

Outside walls

Finish the sides of the house to match the front. Cut the quoins half a brick narrower along the front to fit the strip on the edge of the front panel (Fig 77).

Chimney

Add bricks to the chimney stack to finish at the roof line. Build up a second layer of two bricks, one brick down from the top. Add two chimney pots. Paint the join grey and glue the chimney in place, fixing it to the top of the ceiling.

Porch

This house could have a small porch over the door, with wooden supports on brick piers, or a long verandah, like that on the Edwardian house, but a simple canopy on triangular roof supports like the one shown is very typical and easier to make (Fig 78).

1   Glue a 3 x 16 in (7.6 x 40.6 cm) strip of roofing to three $^3/_8$ in (10 mm) thick triangles 2 in (5 cm) high by 1 $^1/_2$ in (3.8 cm) deep. Place one at each end and centre the third.

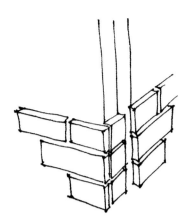

Fig. 72 Extend bricks

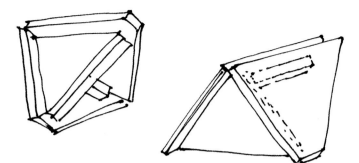

Fig. 75 Assemble dormer roof

Fig. 73 Fit brick quoins

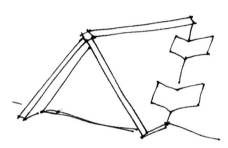

Fig. 76 Fix to roof

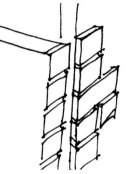

Fig. 77 Short quoins

Fig. 74 Batten dormer triangle

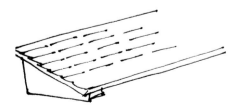

Fig. 78 Porch roof

2 Paint the sides and underneath green and the tiles terracotta, leave to dry, and then glue the porch just below the upstairs windows. You can hold it in place until dry by wedging it against some books and weighting the slope with some more books or kitchen weights.

Outside

The small terrace can be paved with square or crazy paving (irregular, slightly hexagonal slabs). A galvanized dustbin would be well clear of the kitchen; before the days of hygienic plastic bags all the rubbish was tipped straight in. If you have space you can add a greenhouse, a garage (for an Austin 7), a pond with gnomes, a green flock lawn, a white or green picket fence and a sunburst pattern gate.

The Family

The people living in the house can be 1930s or 1940s. The boy in his school uniform could be Richmal Crompton's 'Just William'. The little girl wears a smocked dress, like the one airing in the kitchen. Their mother has a knitted Fair Isle suit and tammy (beret). Father may be on leave from the Army, or wearing sports clothes. The daily, or charwoman, with her scarf tied in front is more 1940s, and the grandmother wears a crepe dress with a V-neck and padded shoulders. Grandfather relaxes with his pipe, in his knitted pullover and carpet slippers.

TUDOR HOUSE FURNISHED IN THE 1990S

CHAPTER EIGHT

Tudor House furnished in the 1990s

Interior of an East Anglian Tudor house with modern furnishings

THIS half-timbered house is typical of those in East Anglia, which were seldom more than two storeys high, apart from an attic. Sometimes cellars were dug out below part of the house for storage. Otherwise the floorboards were laid over joists set in the earth.

This can also be furnished in Jacobean style. It may have started as a hall house, with a central corridor and the main room to the left, the kitchen and services to the right (this time with its own fireplace). Upstairs the rooms would lead off one another. A new partition has been added at the top of the stairs to make a bathroom.

With its clean new paint this house is suitable for modern living. It could be colour washed pale yellow (ochre mixed with white) or pink. True Suffolk pink can be a strong colour. Flowerbeds can be attached to the opening fronts, and a few white doves added to the roof.

Sitting room

The furniture is a mixture of modern and antique. In the sitting room a comfortable sofa and armchair, and an antique leather wing chair are grouped around the open log fire.

An oval dining table is laid with lace table mats (until the 1930s the dining table was always covered with a white damask cloth). There are Regency dining chairs, and a Georgian corner cupboard containing treasured porcelain. A highly polished or varnished oak dresser reminds us of the supposed farmhouse origins. A sofa table stands at the side of the fire, with a modern oil painting above. A small chest of drawers fits beside the door. An antique rug lies in front of the fire.

Hall

In the hall several dogs compete for the basket, and scratch the woven ethnic rug. Popular breeds these days are springer spaniels, a Labrador and a Shih Tzu. An antique

Sitting room, with comfortable sofa and chairs, and some antiques

Hall and oak staircase, with oak chest and green wellies

oak chest is used as a side table, and a primitive painting of a sheep hangs on the wall opposite some modern watercolours. Shaded wall lights are similar to those in the sitting room.

Kitchen

The kitchen has an Aga cooker fitted in the brick fireplace, which has been brightened with white paint. A tall fridge fits in the alcove beside it (not an ideal place, so close to the heat, but it is out of the way) with a wine rack above. Modern units, a sink, cooker and washing machine line the right-hand wall. Fitted cupboards line the other. There is room for more cupboards over the

kitchen units, with a space left above the sink.

The floor is covered in brown and white plastic tiles, which should all be the same size so any border on the sheet should be removed. This probably covers an original brick floor made from local clay.

A traditional pine table, with four scroll back chairs, is used for informal family meals. A wooden bread bin, cornflakes packet, and roast beef straight from the oven all add reality to the room. The baby in a high chair is having his lunch first.

Nursery

Upstairs the children's room is furnished in modern pine, with a bed, chest of drawers, cot and toy cupboard. There is a modern rug, a doll's house, and other toys.

Bathroom

The bathroom has a low cistern toilet, fitted carpet, and shelves of bath salts, etc. There is a chrome soap rack over the bath. The fitted carpet is made from green velvet.

Bedroom

In the master bedroom, a king-size divan has a carved bedhead, a flowered chintz cover (made from the drapes of the four-poster in the Georgian house!) and a wash basin in a modern vanity unit. Some furniture is in antique late Georgian style – a chest of drawers, and a small writing desk. There are also a comfortable chair and modern sofa, a portable TV, bedside light, and flower prints on the wall.

Doll's houses are necessarily rather cramped. It is seldom possible to build a copy of a real house in actual scale; there would be no space to put it. So a 30 ft (9 m) drawing room may be reduced to 15 in (38 cm), and the usual back extensions have to be eliminated. This type of house would have a larger living room, or a separate dining room, in the hall if that were larger, and would certainly run to a second toilet.

It helps to plan the furniture around the family living in the house. The husband may be a country lawyer or bank manager. He has a wife, a small daughter and a baby. The grandfather has come to lunch (no spare bedroom, and only four chairs). The other couple have called in for a drink.

You can add lighting by running the wires along the beams. Remove the plug from a light by pulling the pins out of the plug, then pulling the wires out of the plug. Drill a small hole in the back wall, pull the wire through, then reattach the plug, which can be plugged into a row of sockets allowing you to light each room separately, in a realistic way. If you want a less obtrusive outlet, join the wires to a double screw or spring clip fitting to link the circuit to a 12v transformer.

Master bedroom with king-size bed and portable TV, and modern bathroom with low-level cistern

The nursery has modern pine furniture

The country kitchen has an Aga cooker, fitted pine cupboards, and modern vinyl flooring

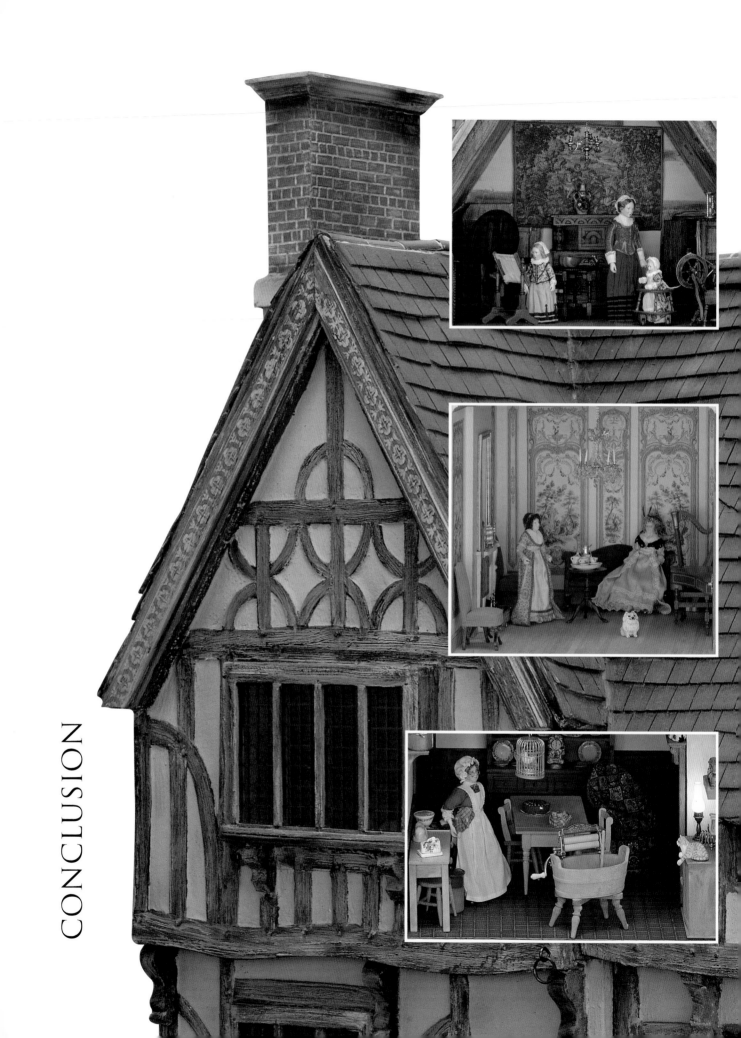

CONCLUSION

CONCLUSION

IN planning these houses, I feel I have been living in them for the past year, researching the period details. In some ways they are a part of my life. My own house is like the stone house, with one more storey. I sometimes stay in an 1840s London house, the model for the Georgian house, complete with black and white hall tiles, but with a basement kitchen. The larger Tudor house is like many I have known and lived in in East Anglia, and the oak furniture is the sort my antique dealer father used to sell.

The 1930s house takes me back to wartime, and the furniture in my granny's house. Edwardian life reminds me of my elegant and eccentric grandma, and grandad's stuffed animal trophies in the hall. Stuffy Victorian houses with drawn curtains make me think of delicate old ladies and their interminable unfinished jig-saws.

I have recently seen houses in France that are still in a complete time warp. Decorative fabric pockets hang on the walls, for knick-knacks and clothes brushes. The fireplaces are filled in with a padded board, wallpapered to match the room, keeping out the damp and the draughts from a house that has been uninhabited for ten years. Two foot (60cm) wide beams have the joists laid across, not set in, the gaps filled with plaster, the ceilings are left bare, the underside of the floorboards stained with soot from centuries of fires. Mirrors hang out at a steep angle, supported on iron pegs in the wall, which I thought was a practice of three hundred years ago.

You can have fun researching your particular period, visiting old houses and looking at furniture in antique shops, where you will often find more variety than in museums. Pick up tips from period dramas on television, even some of the old black and white films were very well researched; in 'Hobson's Choice' John Mills turns off a gas light in the kitchen which has a single flame with no mantel or shade. I could have used this in the 1890s kitchen.

I hope you will find inspiration to create your own period world. I do not claim to be an expert, but hope to have supplied the guidelines to the various styles which you can now adapt.

Happy collecting!

PUBLICATIONS

Magazines UK

International Dolls' House News
Nexus Special Interests Ltd
Nexus House
Azalea Drive
Swanley
Kent BR8 8HU
(Established 1967.Bi-monthly.)

Dolls' House World
Ashdown Publishing Ltd
Avalon Court
Star Road
Partridge Green
West Sussex RH13 8RY
(Established 1989. Monthly.)

Dolls House and Miniature Scene
EMF Publishing
EMF House
5-7 Elm Park
Ferring
West Sussex BN12 5RN
(Established 1992. Monthly.)

The Dolls' House Magazine
Guild of Master Craftsman
   Publications Ltd
166 High Street
Lewes
East Sussex BN7 1XU
(Established 1998. Monthly.)

Magazines USA

Dollhouse Miniatures
Kalmbach Publishing Co.
PO Box 1612
Waukeshka
WI 53187
USA
(Established 1997. Monthly.)

Miniature Collector
Scott Publications
30596 Eight Mile
Livonia
MI 48152-1798
USA
(Established 1974. Quarterly.)

Books

Build a Doll's House
Michal Morse, Batsford

Furnish a Doll's House
Michal Morse, Batsford

Authentic Decor
*Peter Thornton, Weidenfeld and
   Nicolson*

English Furniture
John Bly, Shire

Mrs Beeton's Book of Household
Management

There are many useful reference
books available about furniture,
architecture, costume, and the
specialist Shire books, such as
Domestic Bygones.

Fairs

The London Dollshouse Festival
Kensington Town Hall
London W8
early May
(all enquiries to:
25 Priory Walk
Kew
Richmond
Surrey TW9 3DQ)

Miniatura
The National Exhibition Centre
Birmingham
(Spring & Autumn)
(all enquiries:
41 Eastbourne Avenue
Hodge Hill
Birmingham B34 6AR)

There are many other fairs every
weekend, listed in the specialist
magazines. Enclose a stamped
addressed envelope or International
Reply Coupon with any enquiry to
ensure a reply.

Specialist shops (UK)

The Dolls House
Market Place
Northleach, nr Cheltenham
Glos GL54 3EJ
Tel/Fax: 01451 860431
(Established by Michal Morse, 1971)

Andrew's Miniature World
16 Northumberland Place
Teignmouth
Devon PQ14 8BZ
Tel/Fax: 01626 779672

Church Street Miniatures
26 Church Street
Godalming
Surrey GU7 1EW
Tel: 01483 427023

Goodies
11 East Street
Coggeshall
Essex CO6 1SH
Tel: 01376 562885

Guiscard Miniatures
7 Princes Street
Perth
Perthshire PH
Tel: 01738 446318

The London Dolls House Co
29 Covent Garden Market
London WC2E 8RE
Tel: 0171 240 8681
(Established 1995)

The Miniature Scene of York
42 Fossgate
York Y01 2TF
Tel: 01904 638265

SUPPLIERS

Specialist shops (USA)

Angela's Miniature World
2237 Ventura Blv
Camarillo
CA 93010
Tel: (805) 482 2219

Dollhouse Antics
1343 Madison Avenue
  (at 94th St.)
New York
NY 10128
Tel: (212) 876 2288

It's a Small World
560 Green Bay Road
Winnetka
IL 60093
Tel: (708) 446 8399

Petite Elite Miniature Museum
  & Shop
Carole & Barry Kaye Museum of
  Miniatures
5900 Wiltshire Blv
Los Angeles
CA 90036
Tel: (213) 937 7766

Washington Doll's House & Toy
  Museum
Museum Shop
5236 44th Street NW
Washington
DC 20015
Tel: (202) 244 0024

See the magazines for listings of
many more shops.

Specialist suppliers

Anglesey Dolls Houses
5a Penhros Industrial Estate
Holyhead
Anglesey LL65 2UQ
Tel: 01407 763511
  Bay windows, doors,
  mouldings etc.

Reuben Barrows
30 Wolsey Gardens
Hainault
Ilford
Essex IG62SN
Tel: 01992 719593
  Wall, floor and roof cladding

Blackwells of Hawkwell
The Old Maltings
5 Weir Pond Road
Rochford
Essex SS4 1AH
Tel: 01702 544211
DIY Supplies

From Little Acorns
2 Summerholme
de la Warr Parade
Bexhill-on-Sea
East Sussex TN 40 1NR
Tel: 01424 731561
  Moulded wall, floor & roof
  cladding, printed vinyl flooring

W.Hobby Ltd
Knights Hill Square
London SE27 0HH
Tel: 0181 761 4244
DIY Supplies

Dolls houses by Vic Newey, Mick Hoyle, Sid Cooke, Timberlina, Barrie Osborne,
others adapted by the author from kits of Build a Dolls House plans.

INDEX